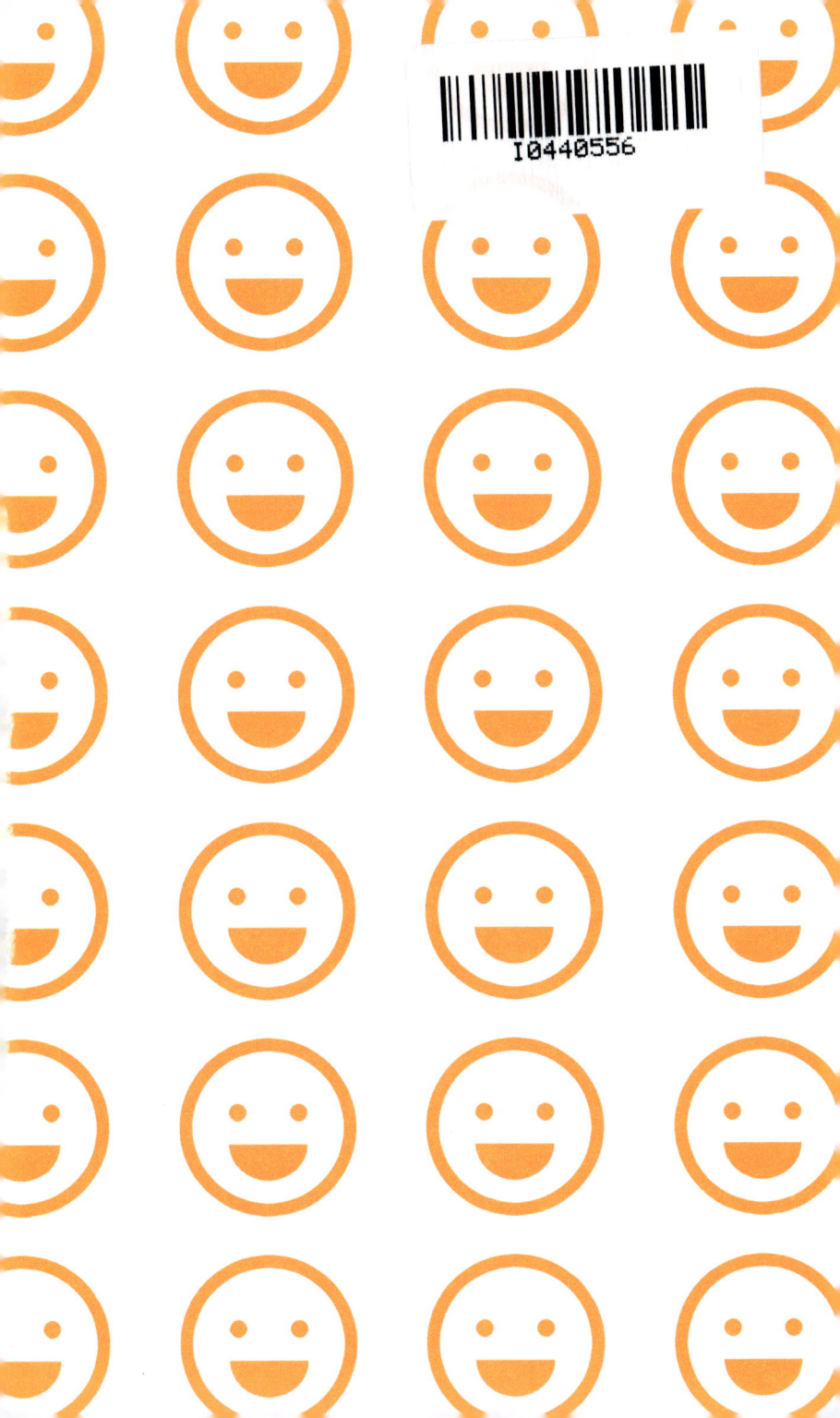

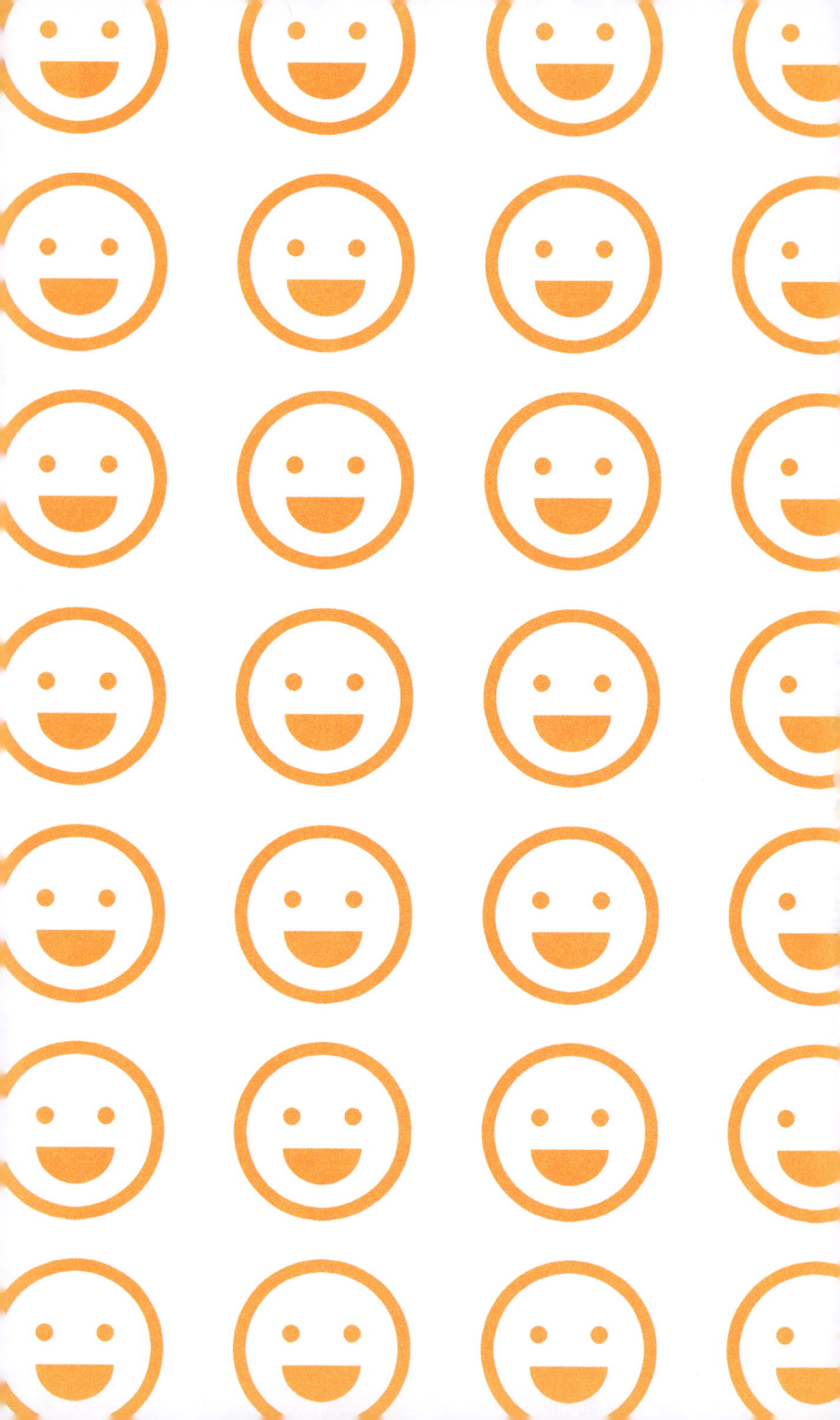

DRIVE FAST DON'T STOP

BOOK EIGHT

ANOTHER RANDOM ASSORTMENT

FAST DON

FAST DON"

E FAST DON'T,

VE FAST DON'T S

RIVE FAST DON'T STO

DRIVE FAST DON'T STOP

DRIVE FAST DON'T STOP

FAST DON'T

FAST DON'T

E FAST DON'T

VE FAST DON'T ST

RIVE FAST DON'T STO

DRIVE FAST DON'T STOP

DRIVE FAST DON'T STOP

UTOMÓVIL

UTOMÓVIL

AUTOMÓVILES

AUTOMÓVILES

AUTOMÓVILES

AUTOMÓVILES

AUTOMÓVILES

UTOMÓVILE

UTOMÓVILE

AUTOMÓVILES

AUTOMÓVILES

AUTOMÓVILES

AUTOMÓVILES

AUTOMÓVILES

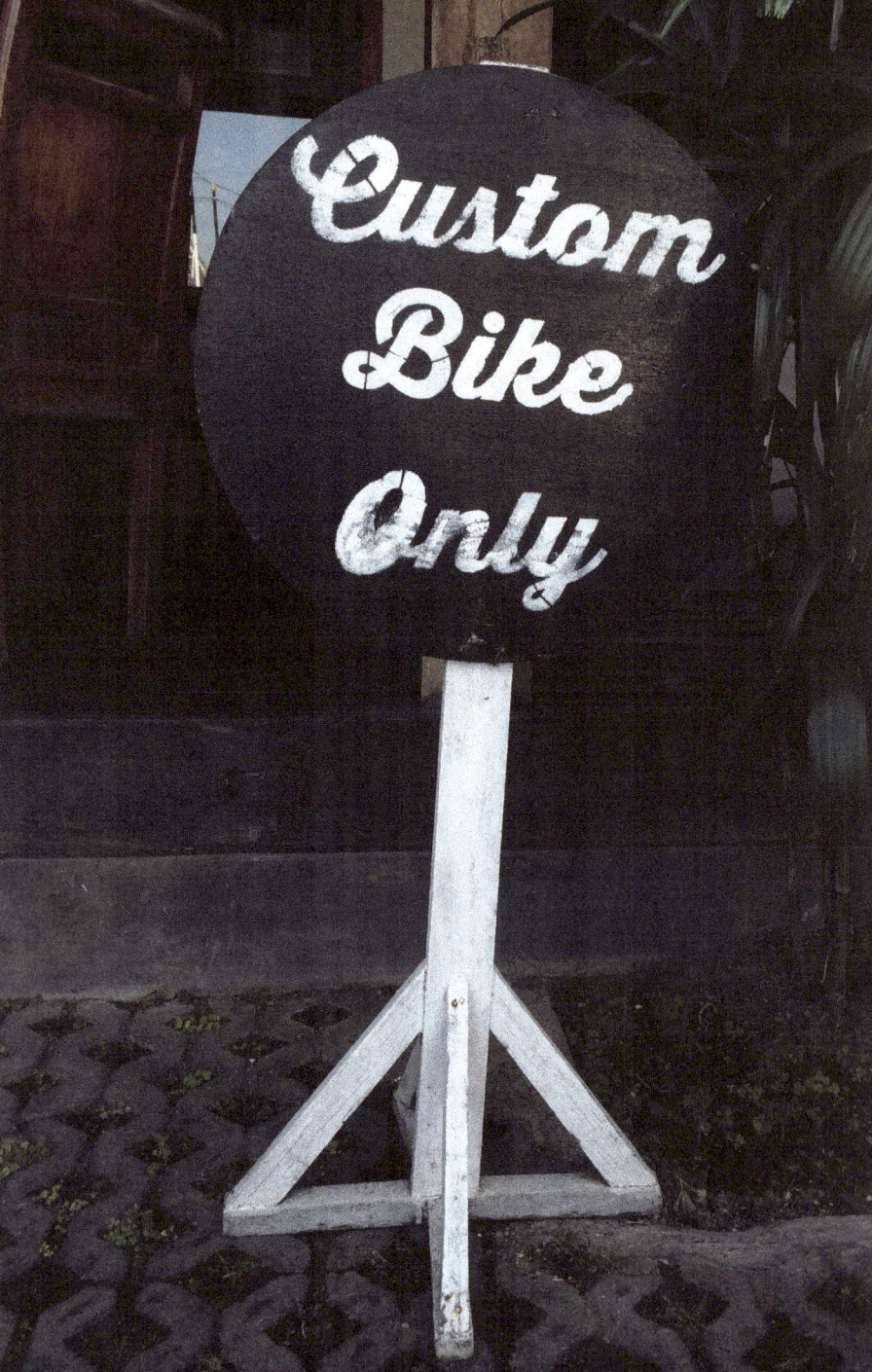

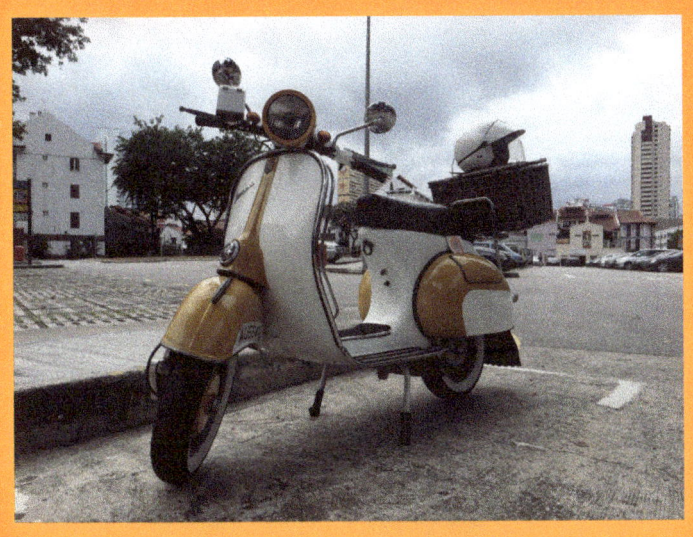

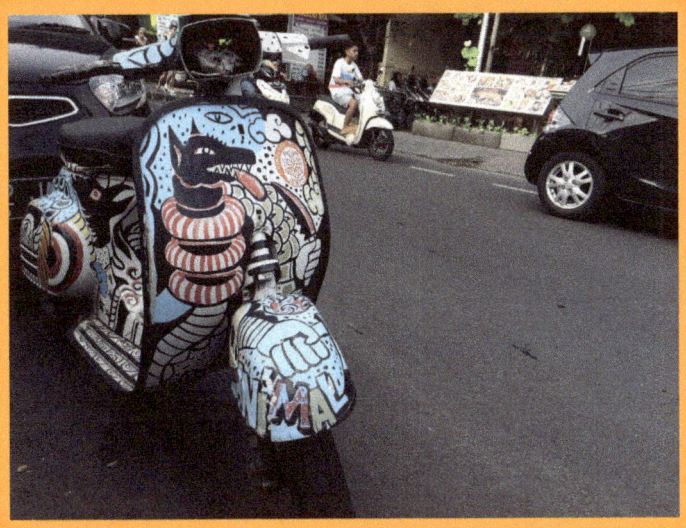

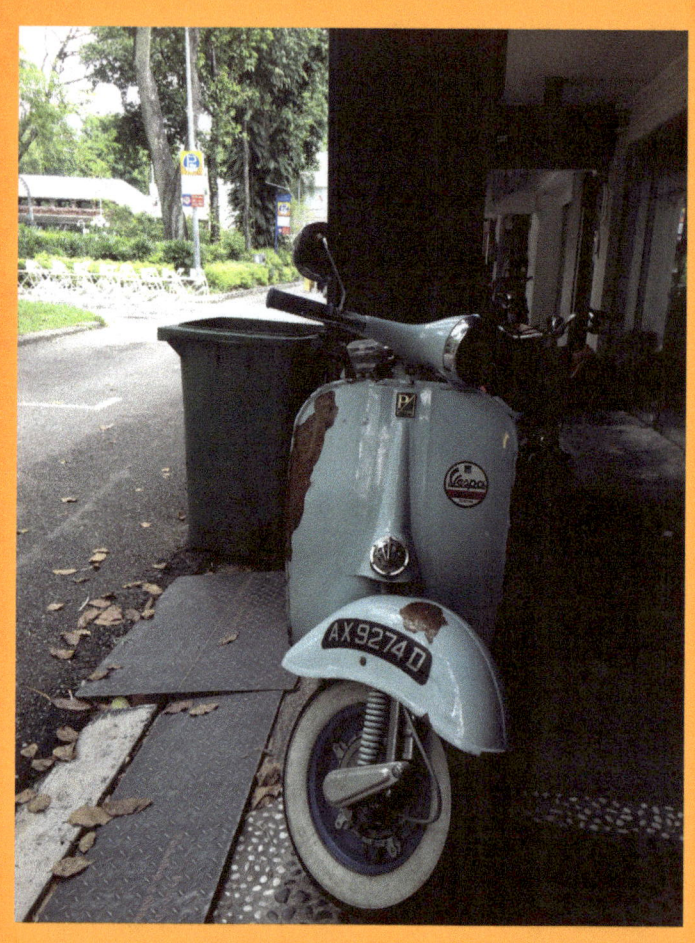

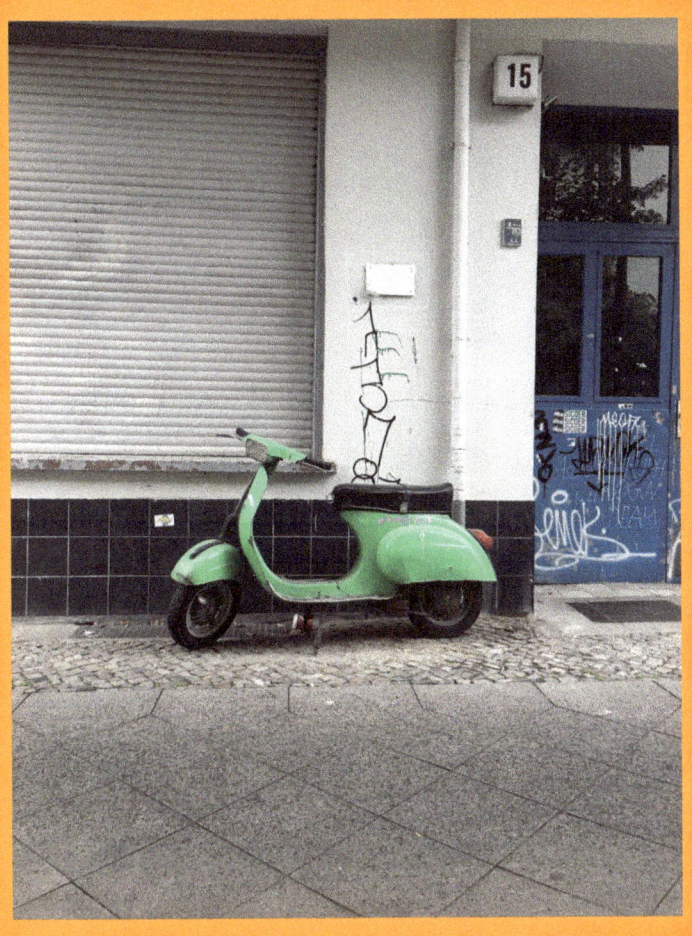

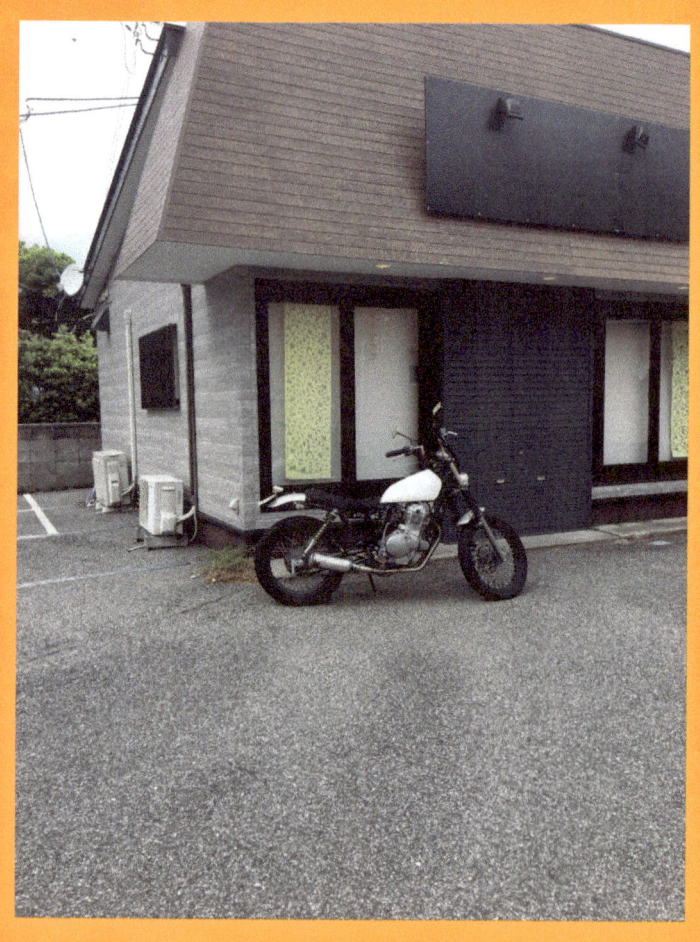

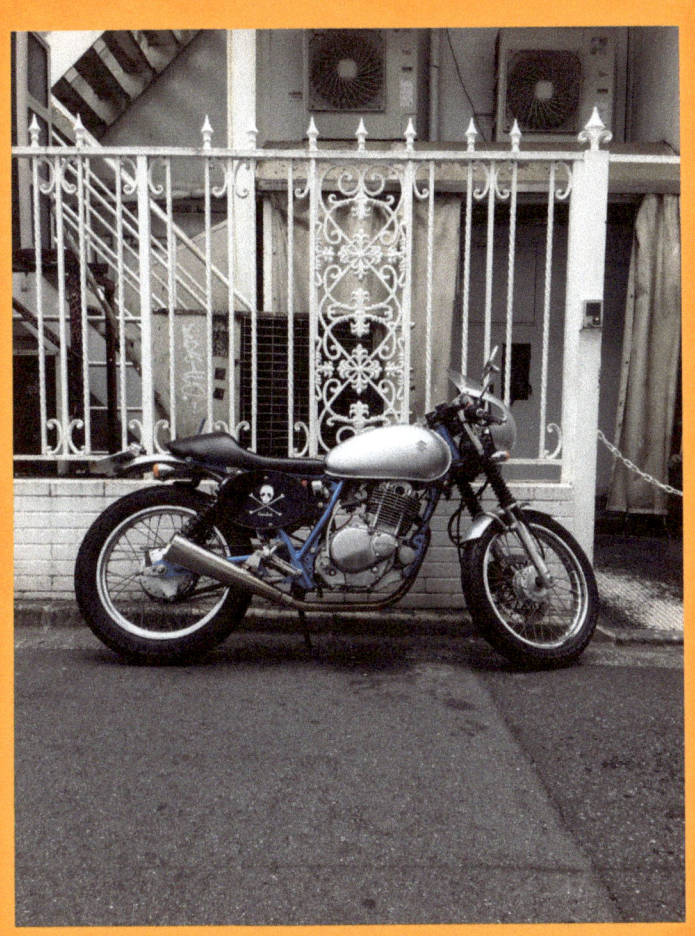

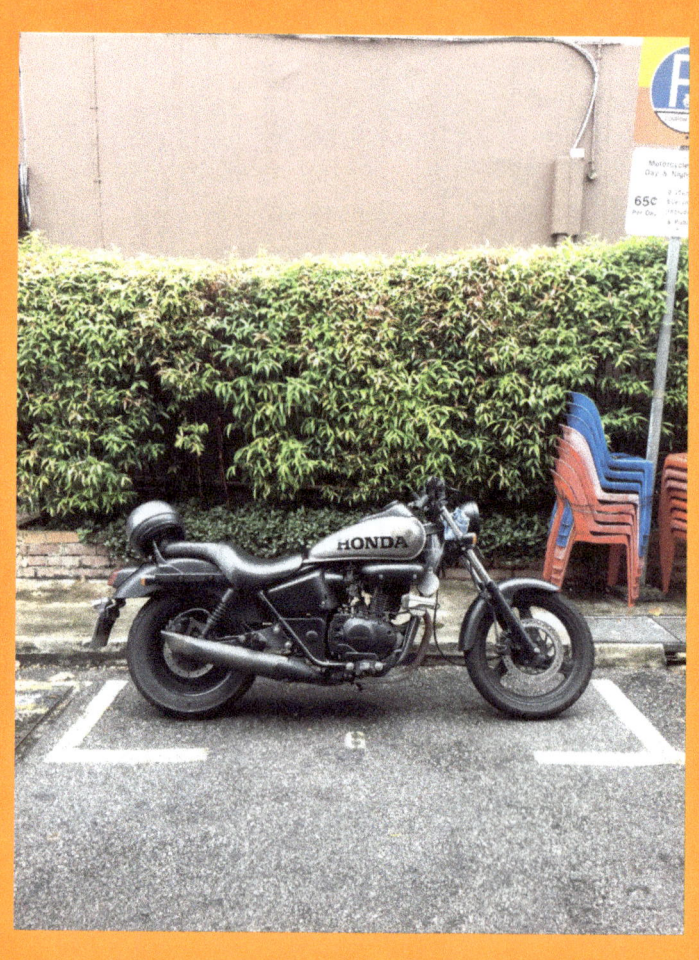

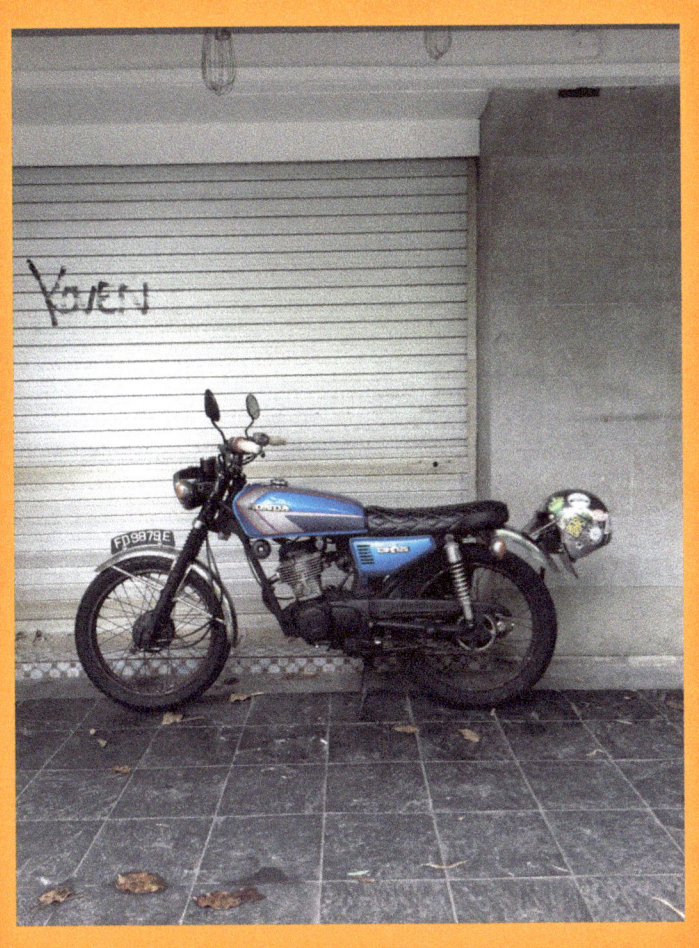

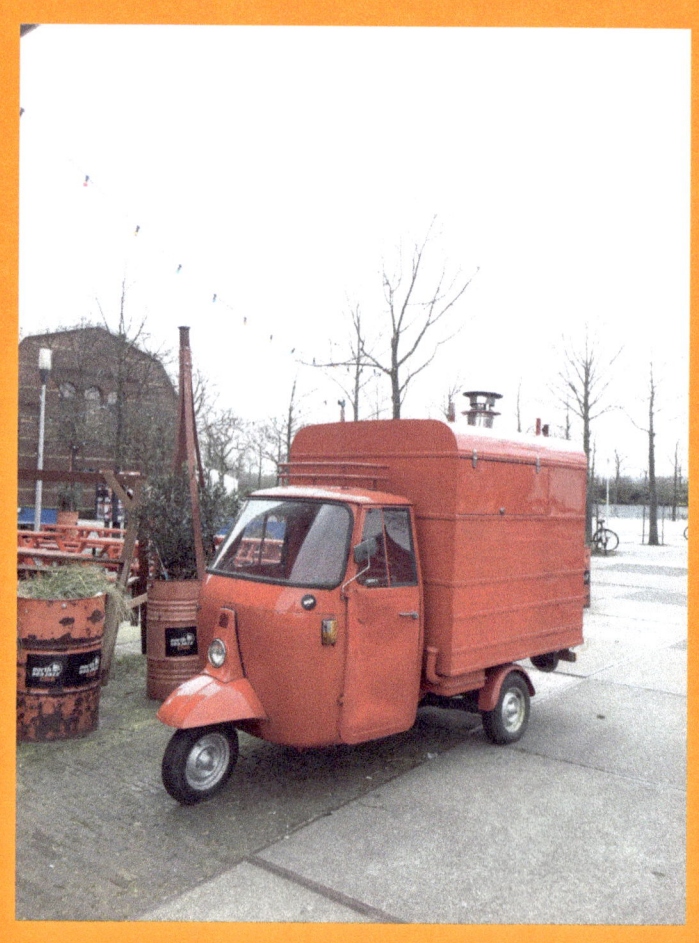

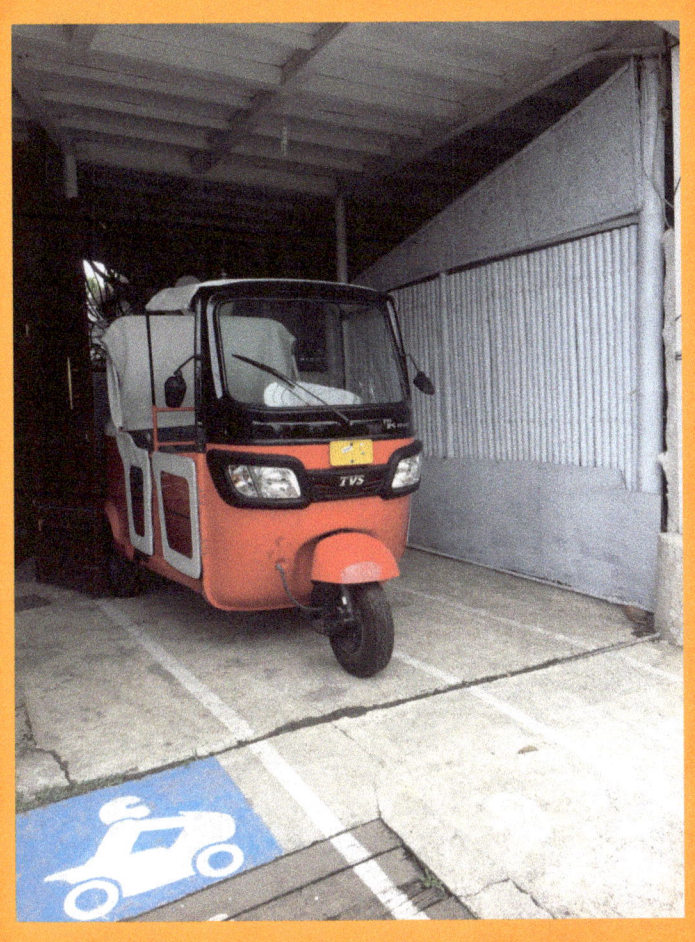

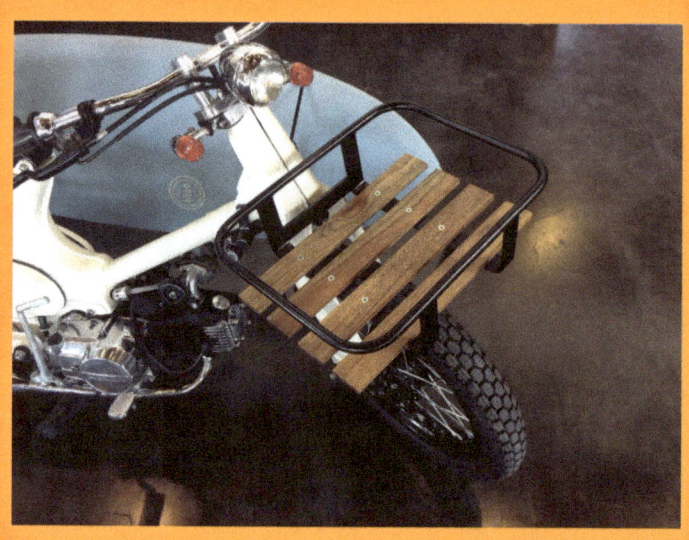

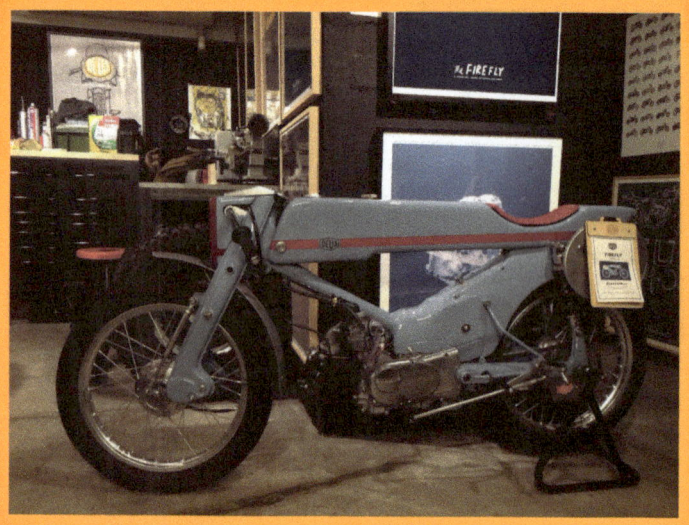

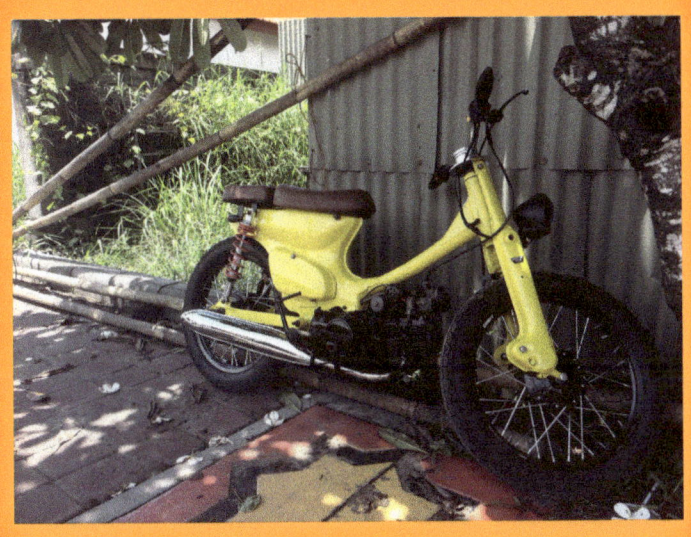

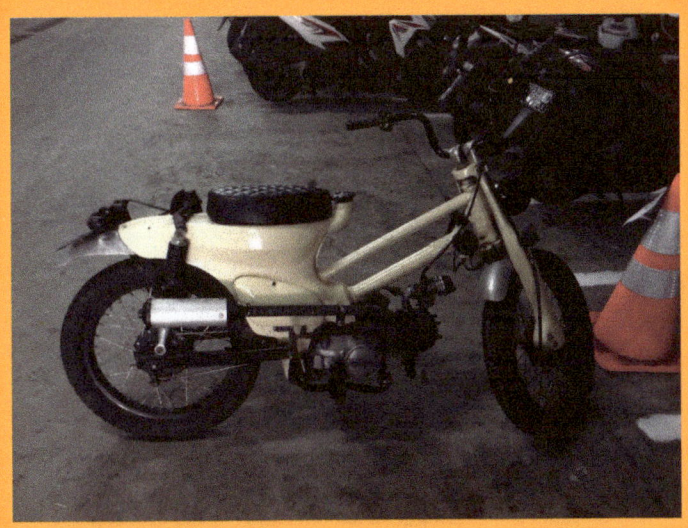

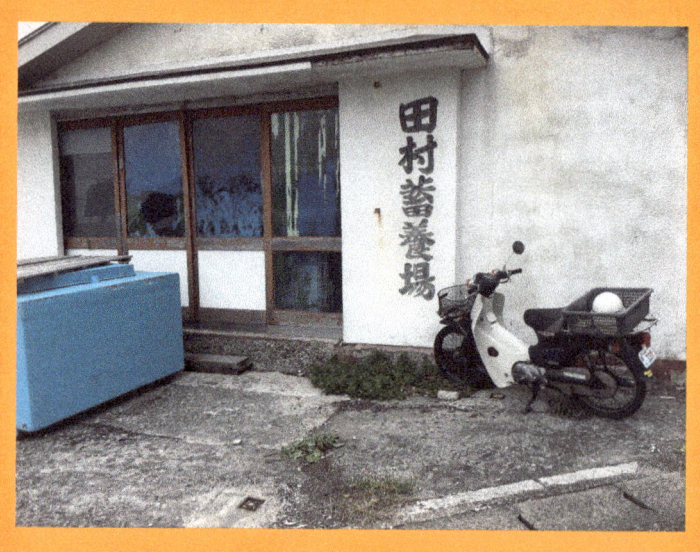

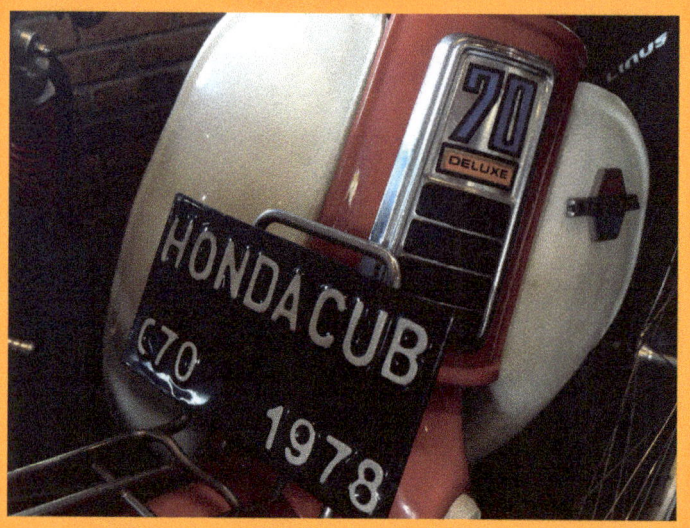

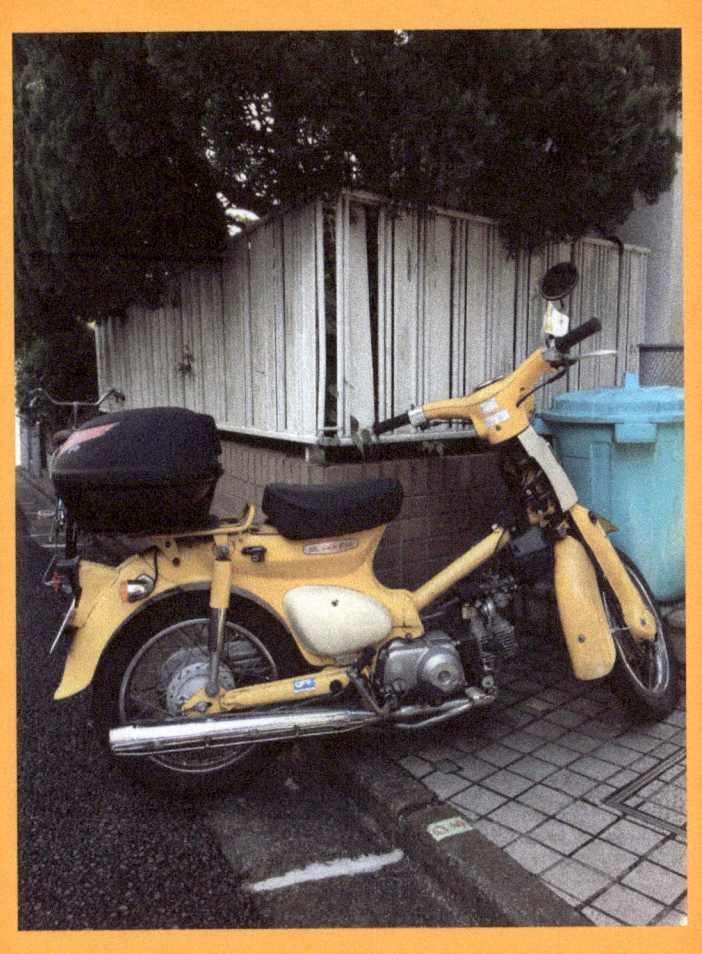

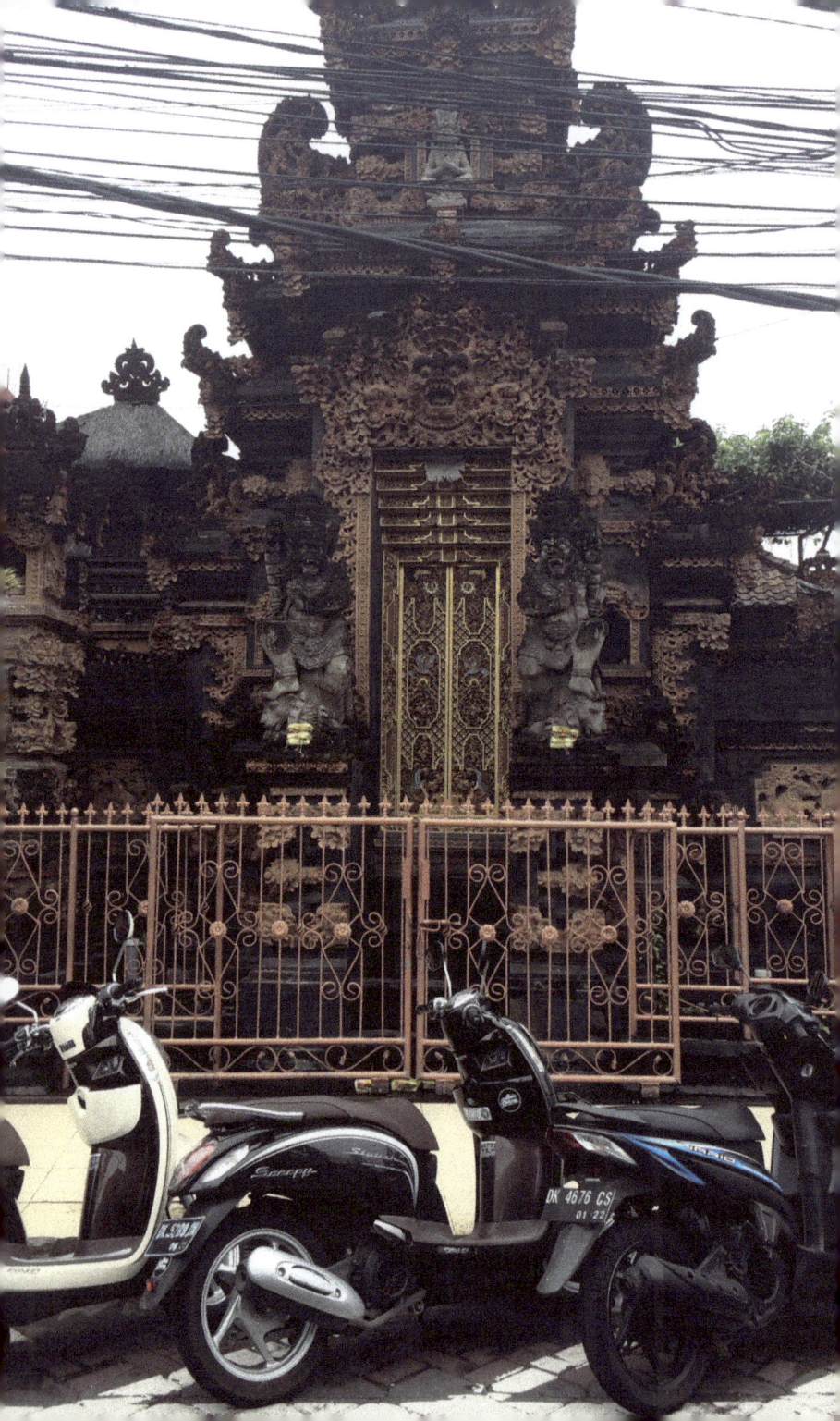

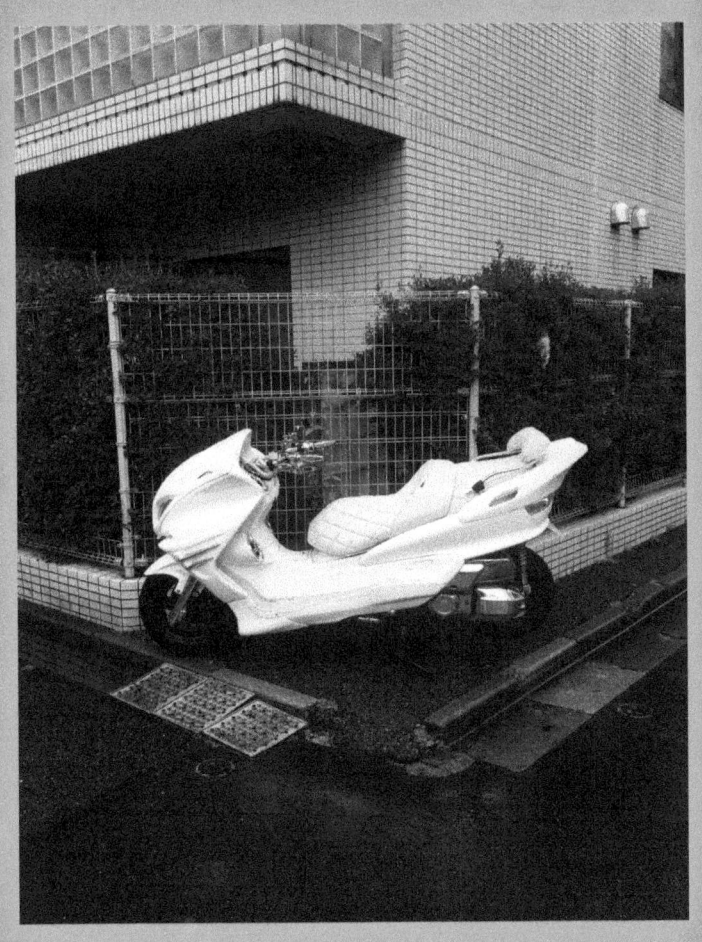

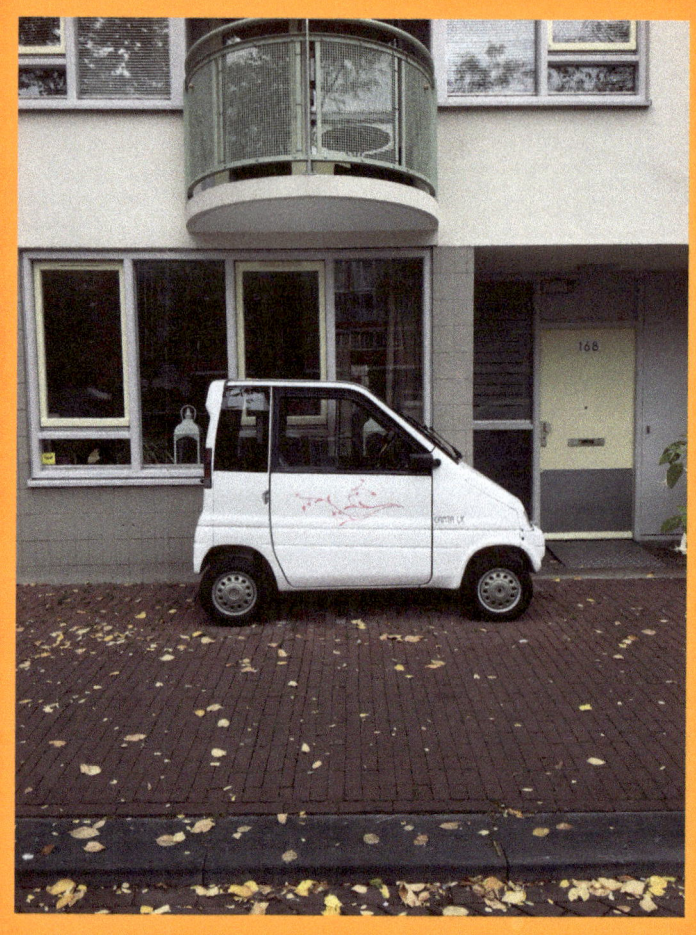

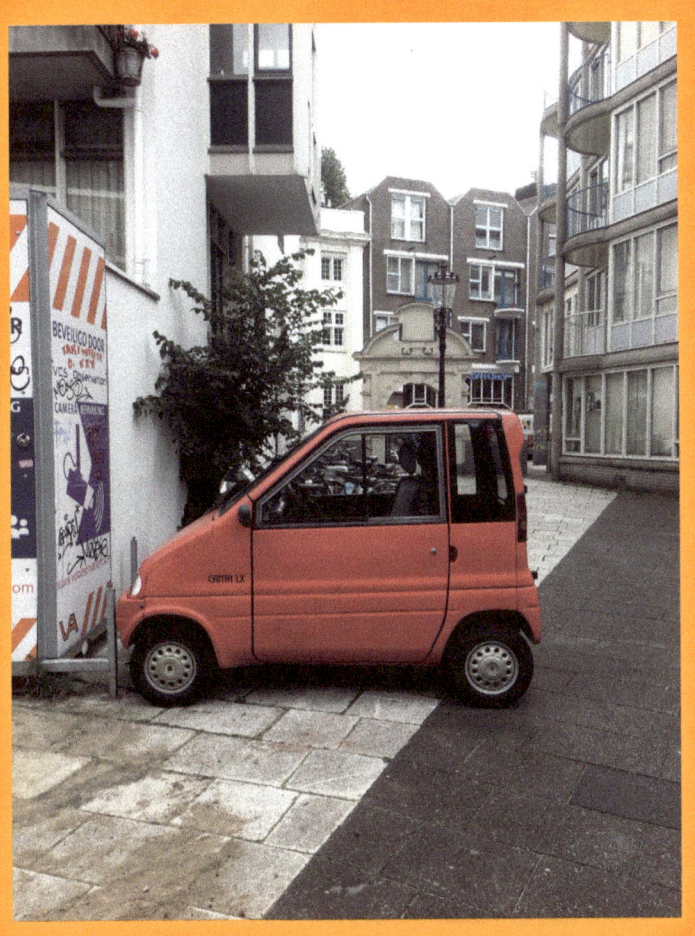

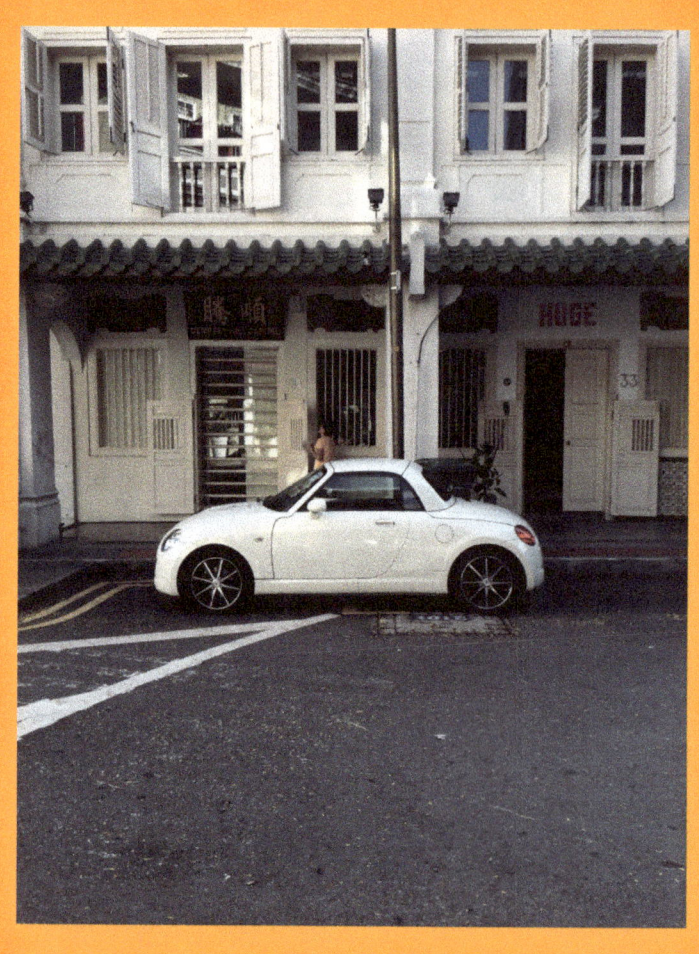

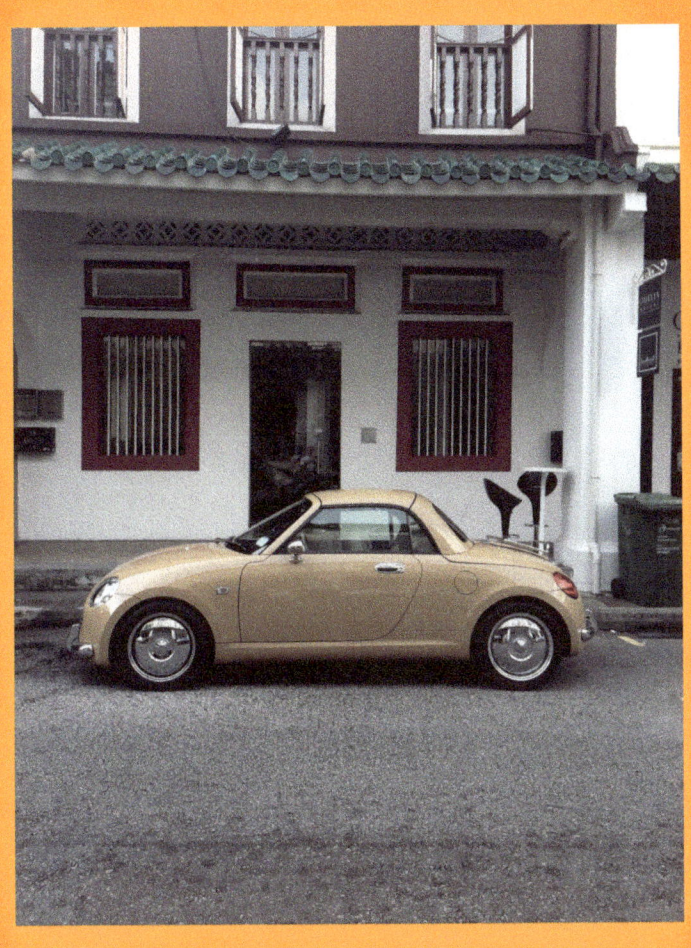

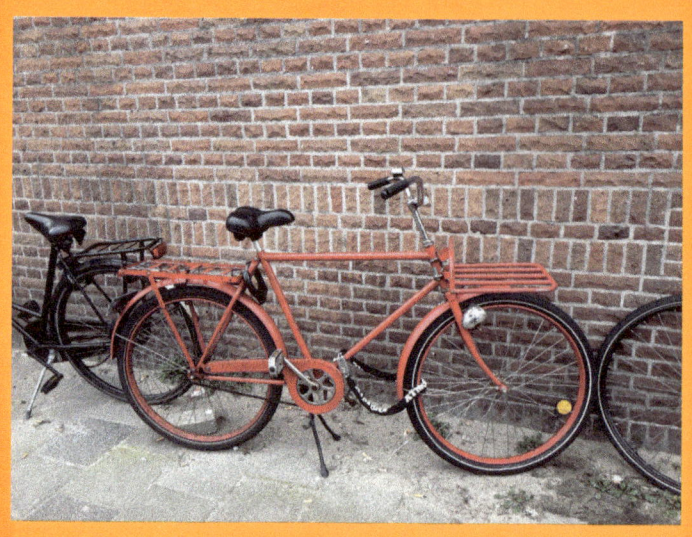

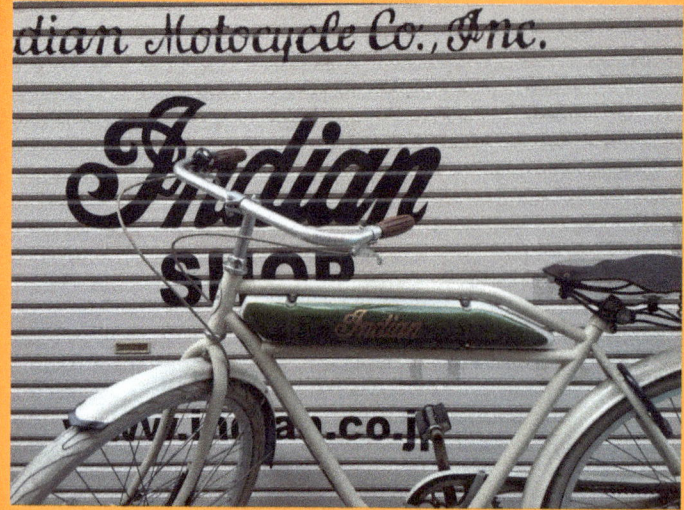

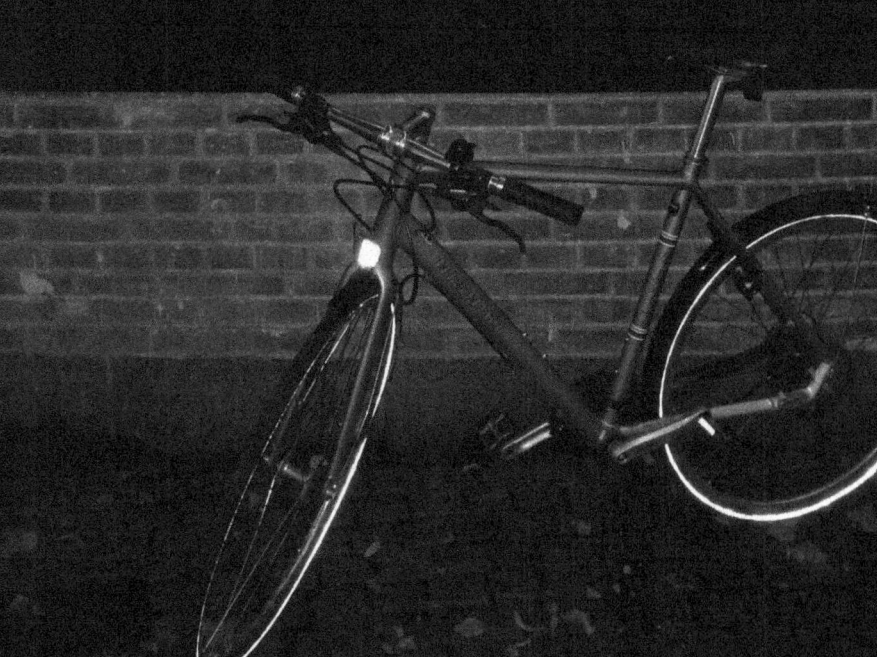

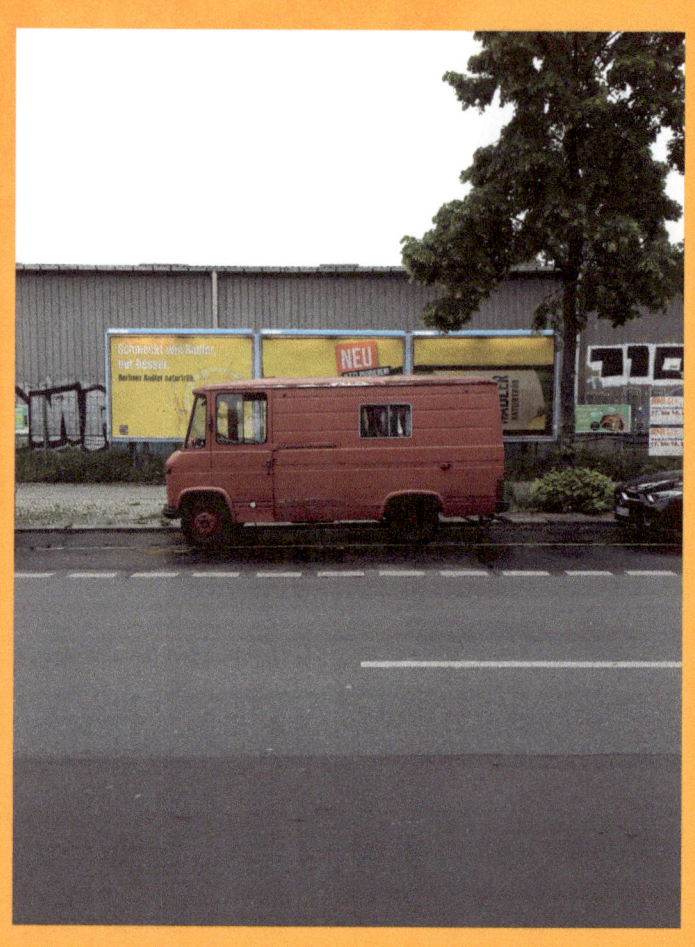

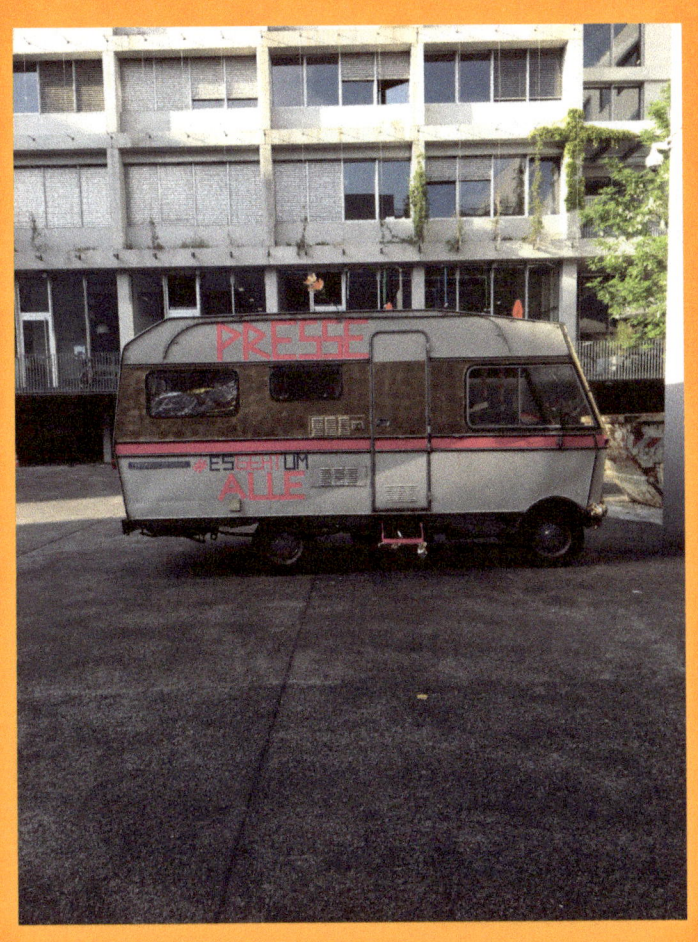

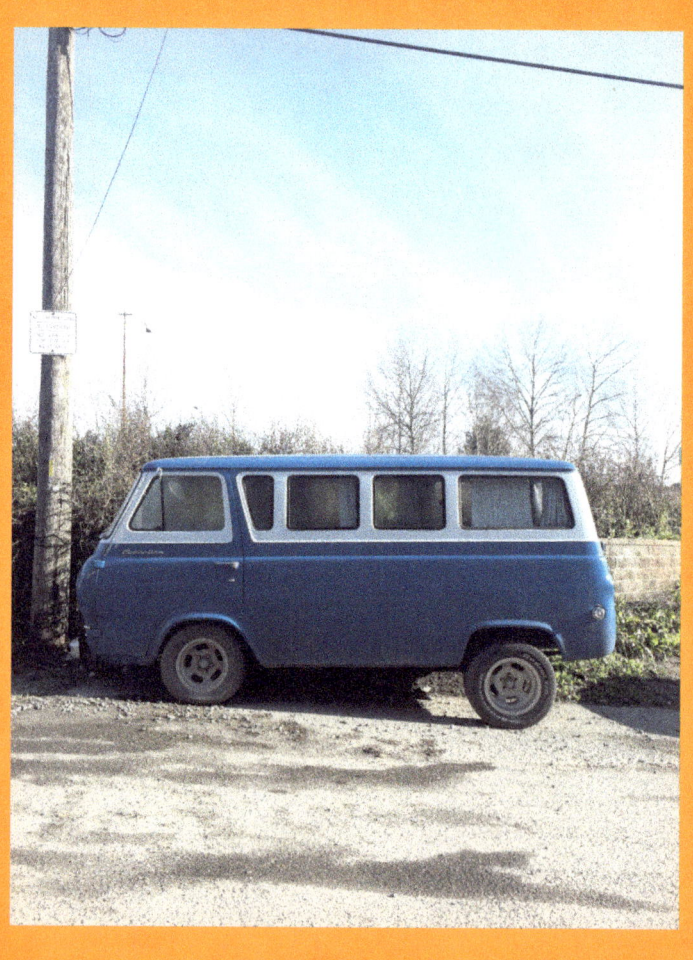

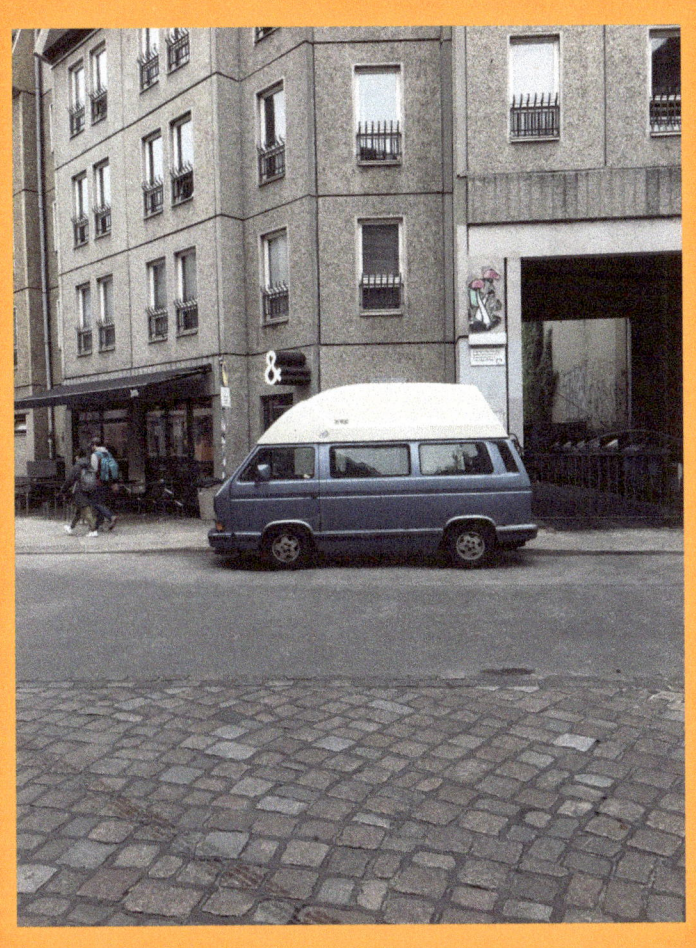

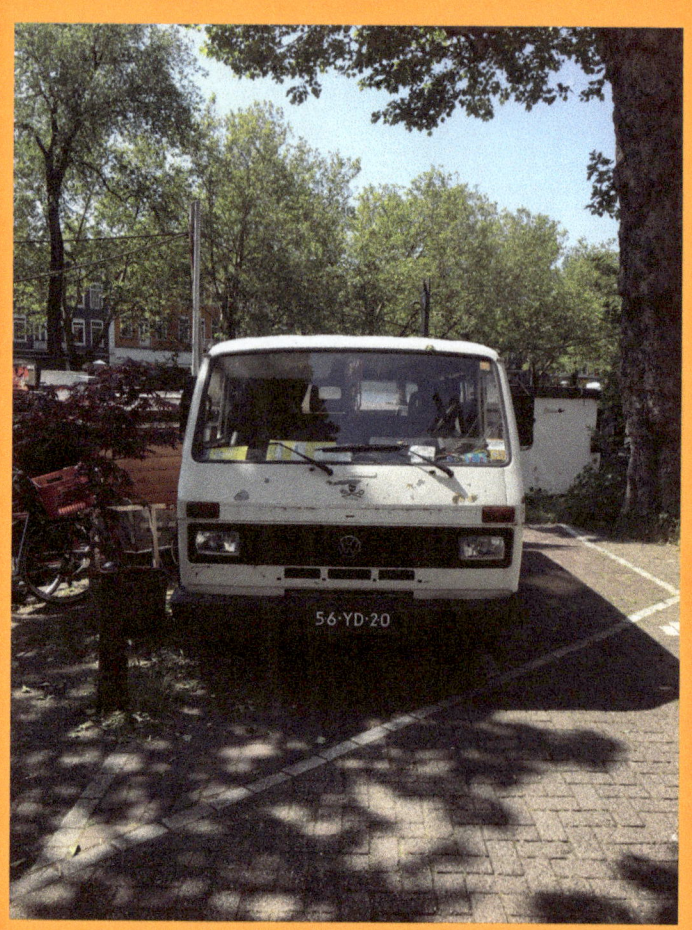

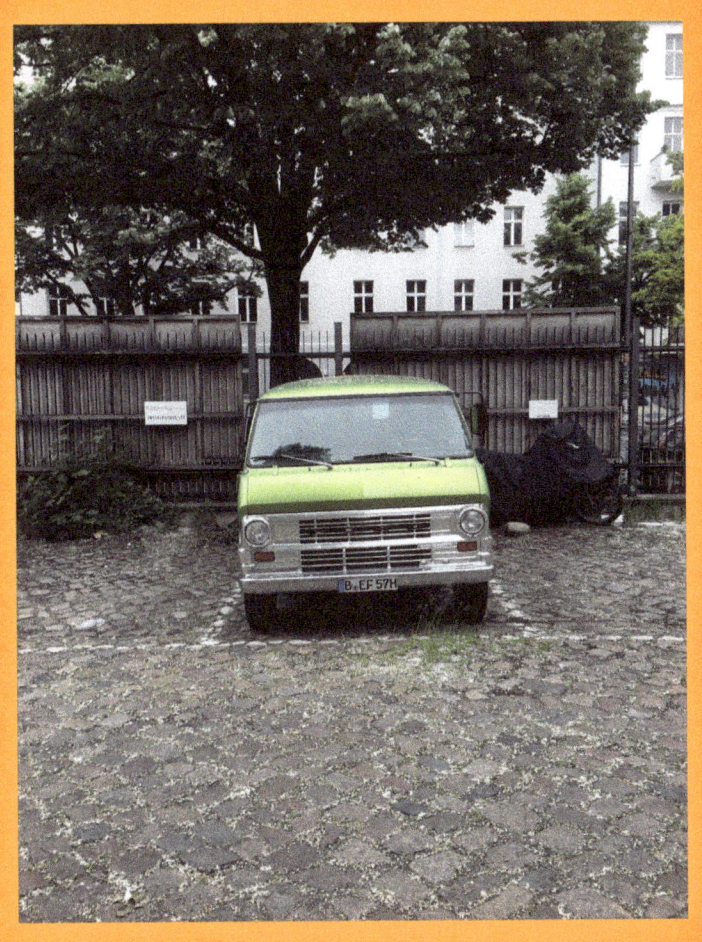

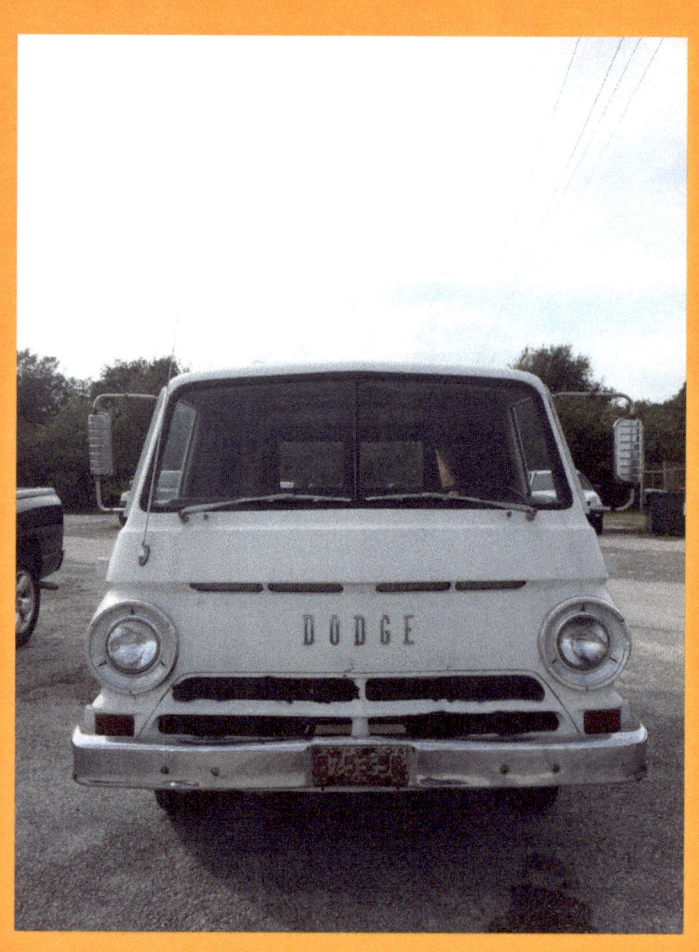

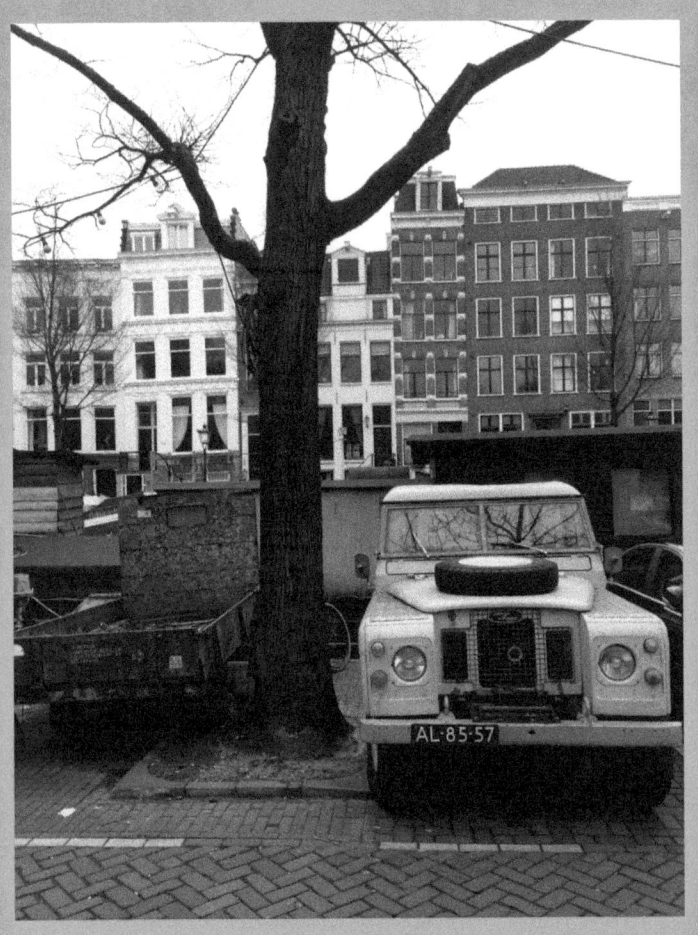

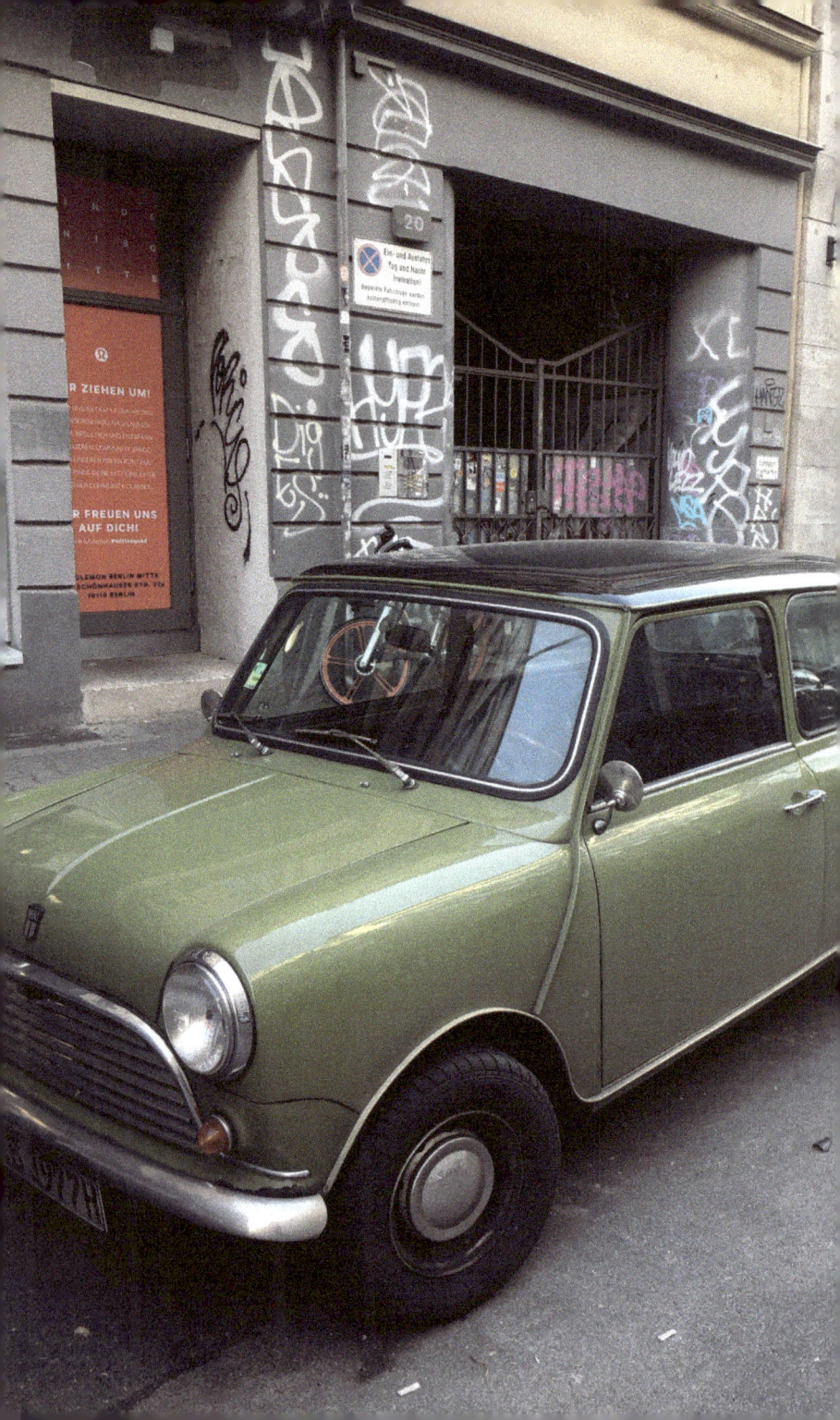

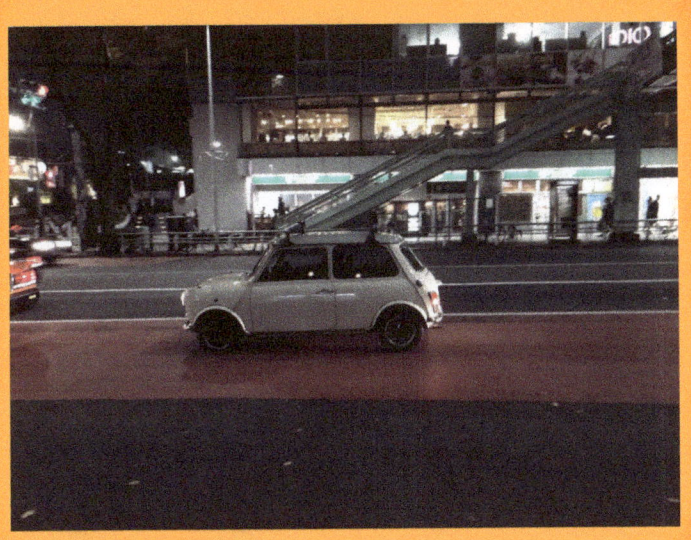

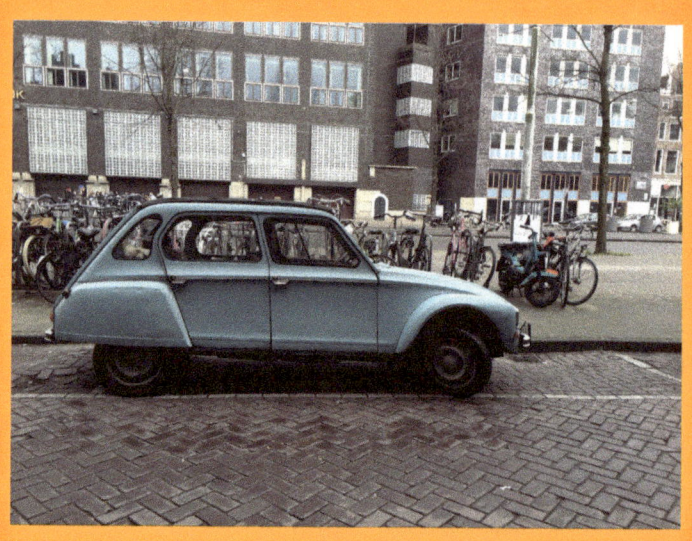

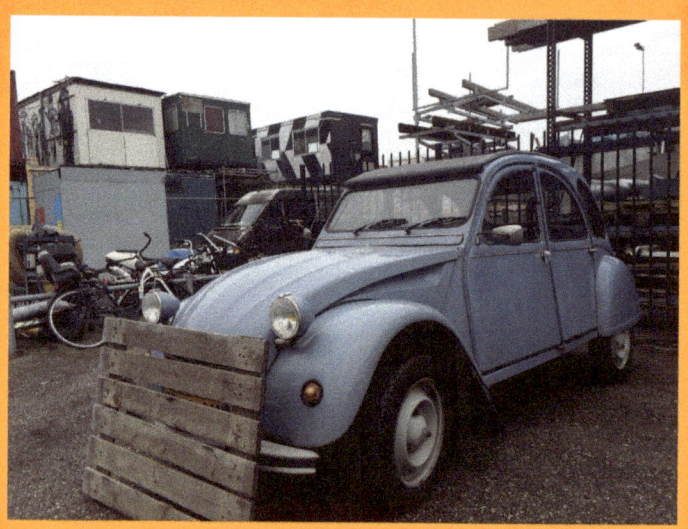

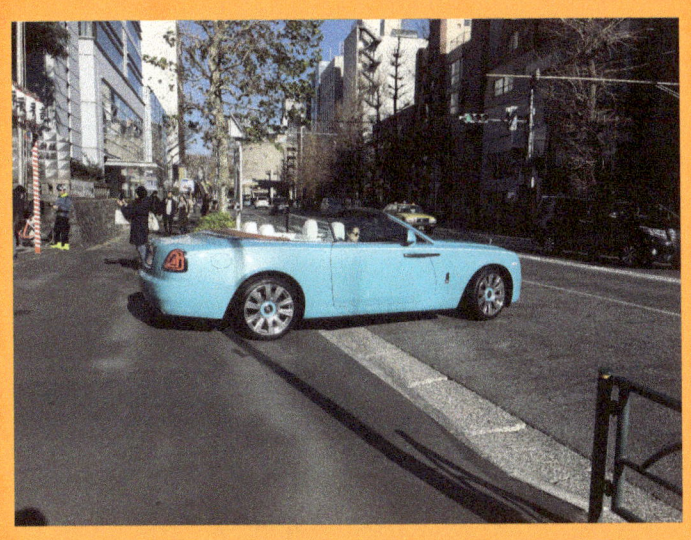

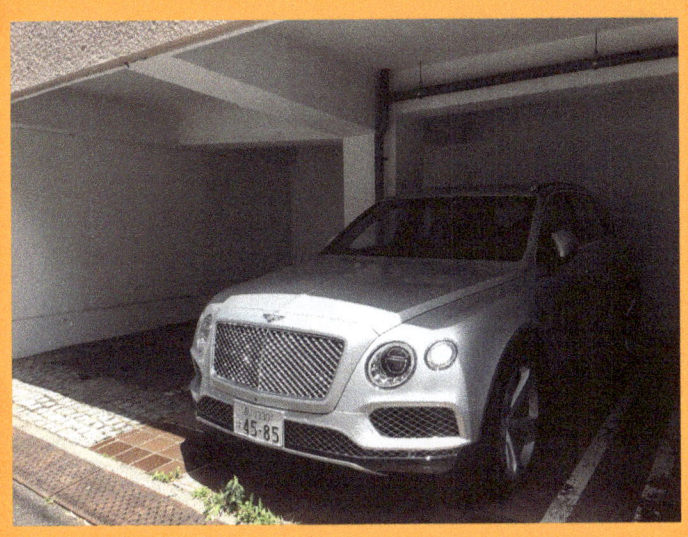

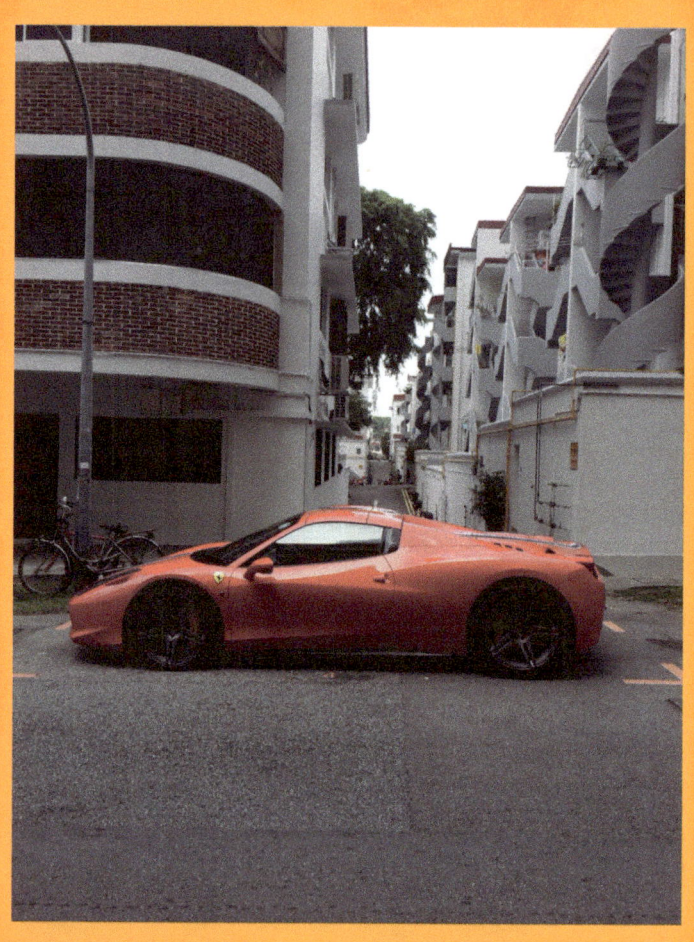

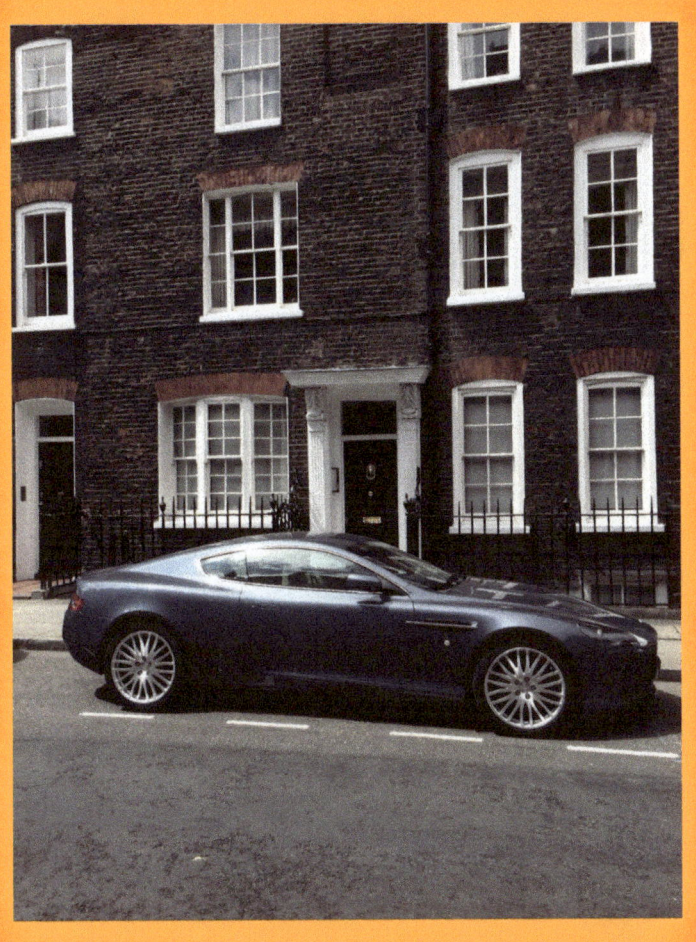

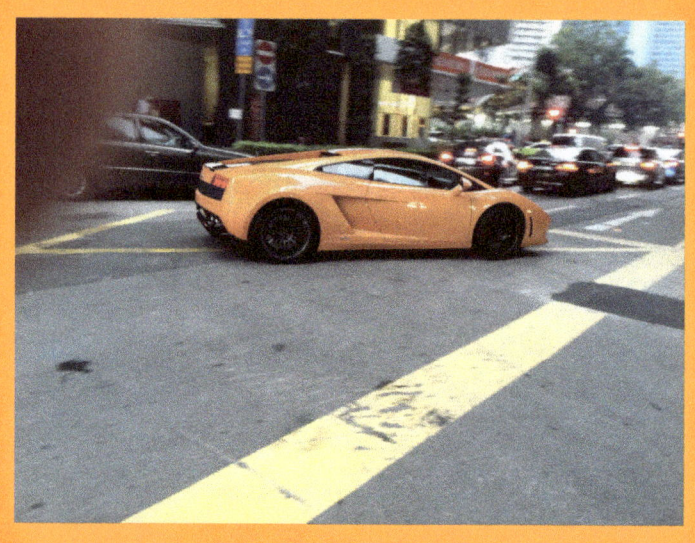

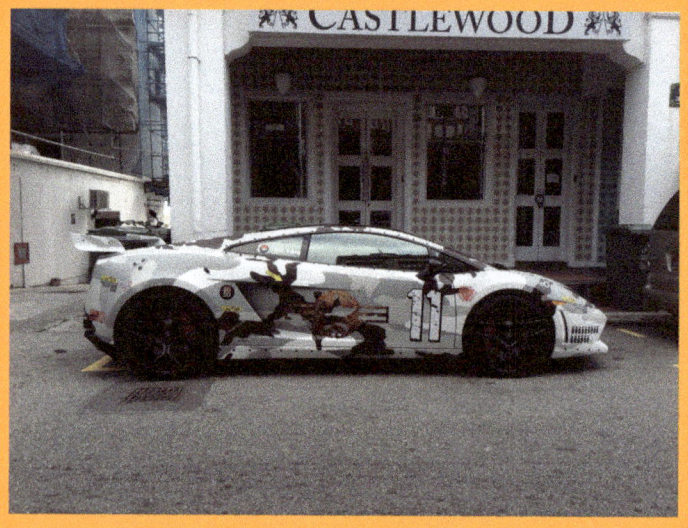

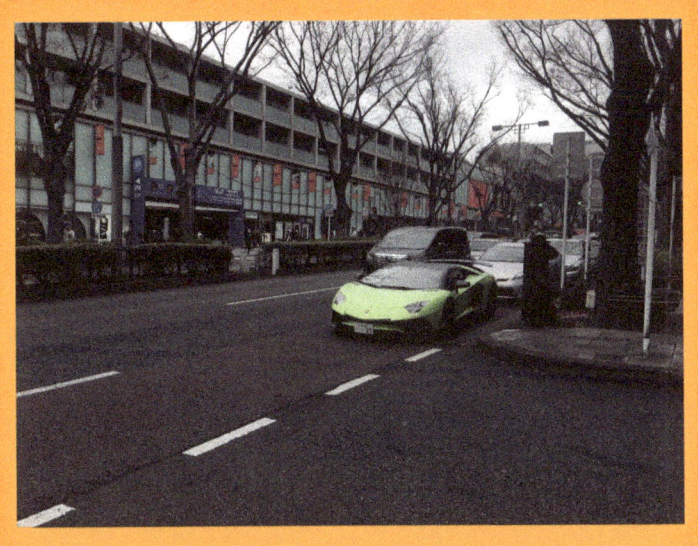

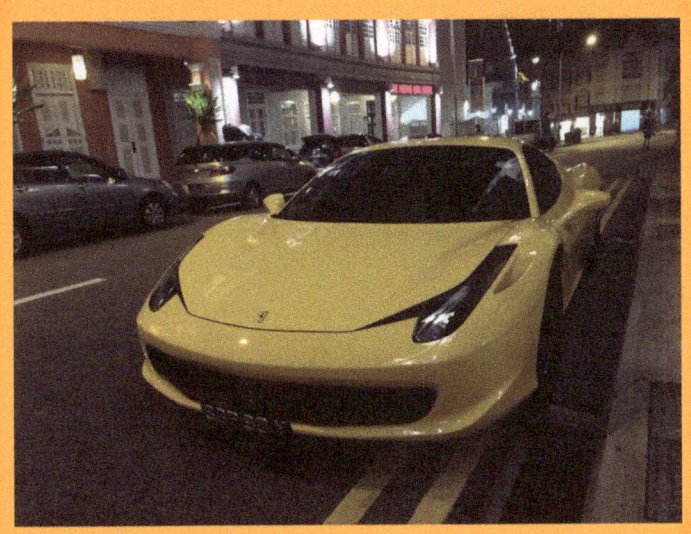

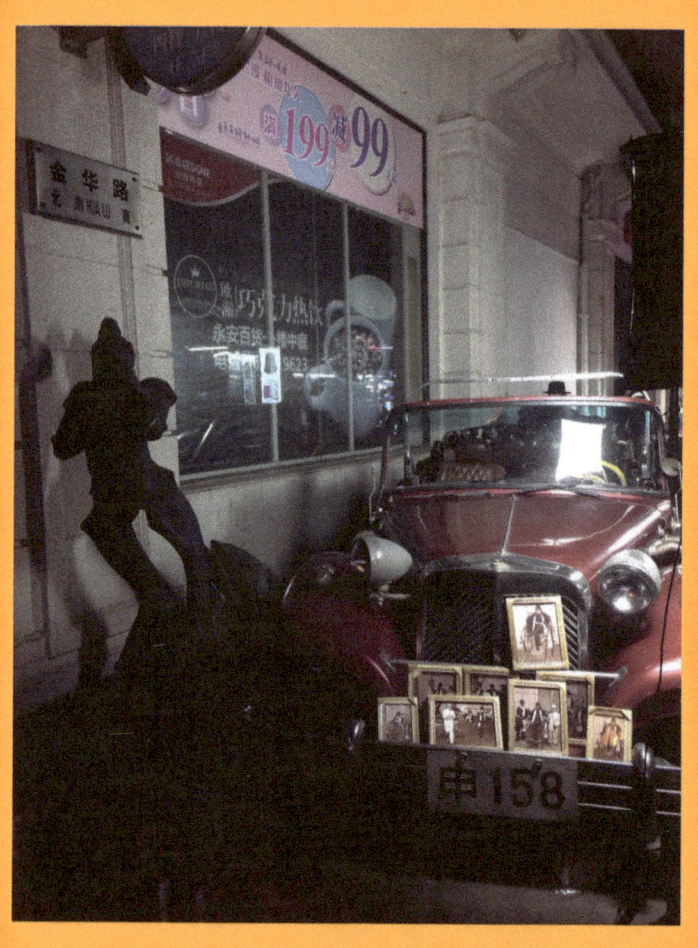

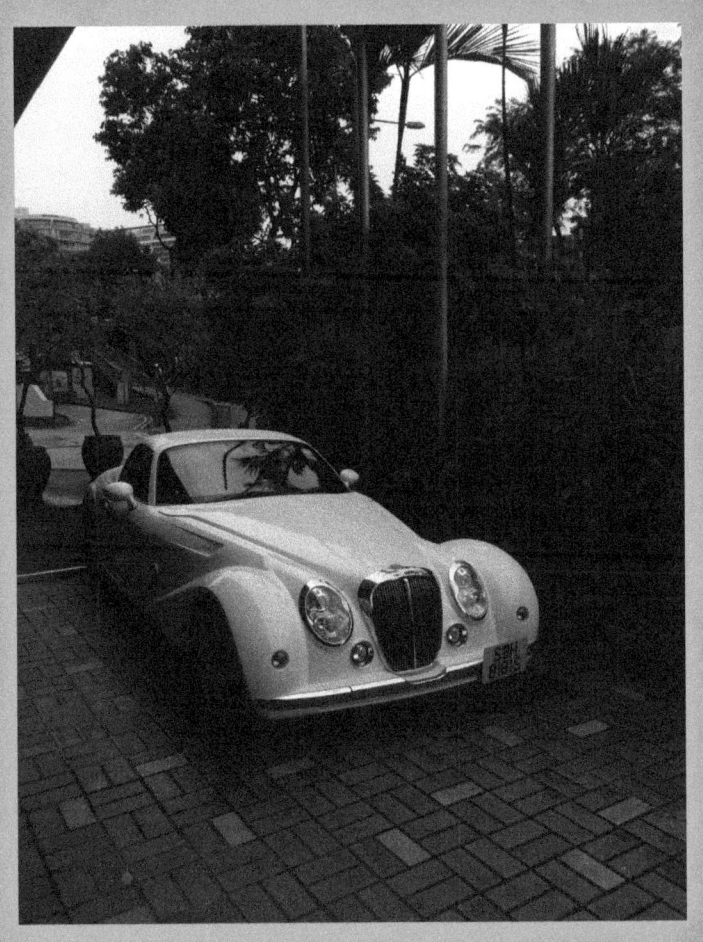

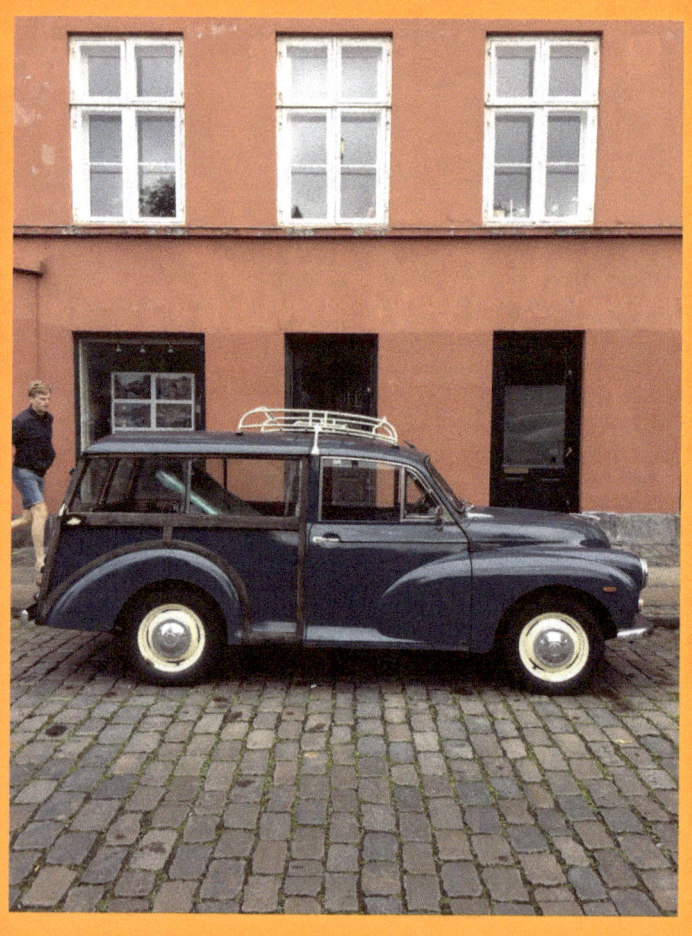

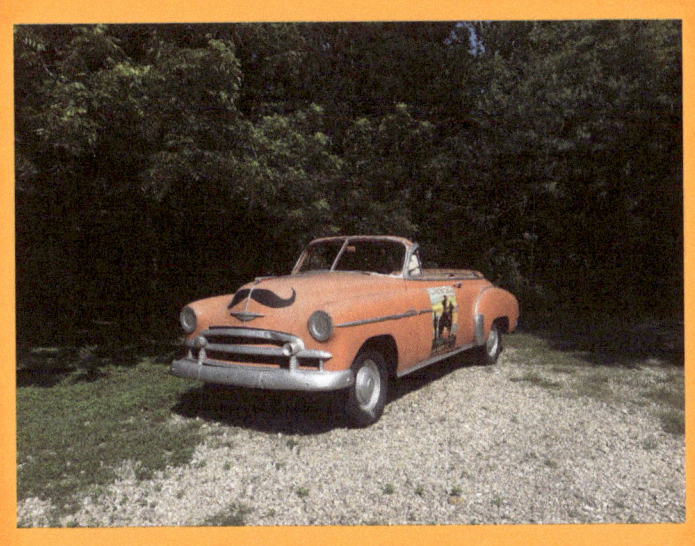

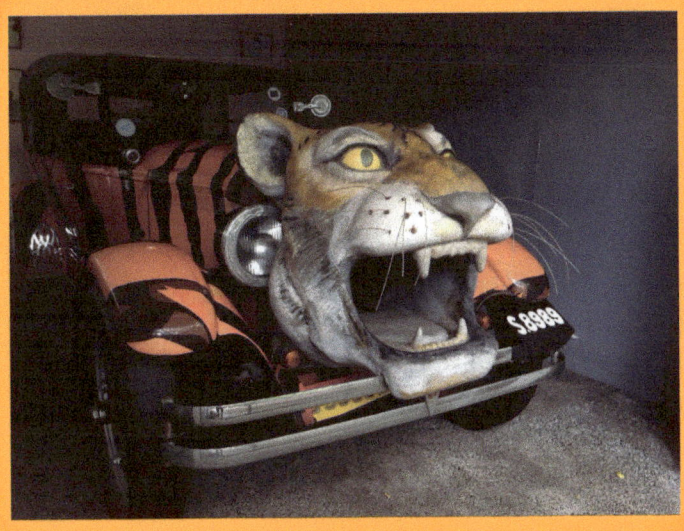

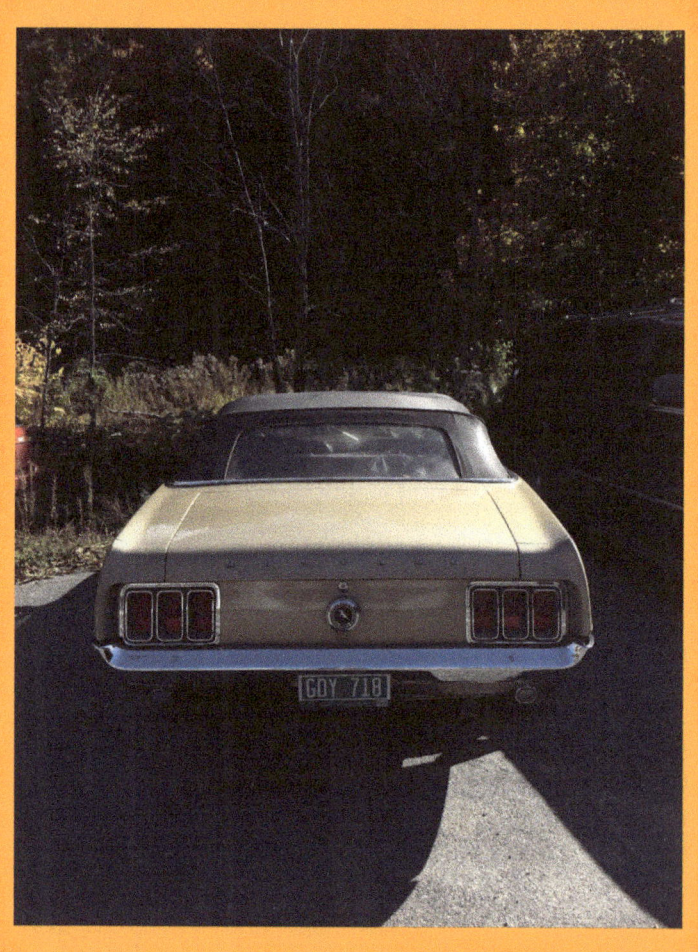

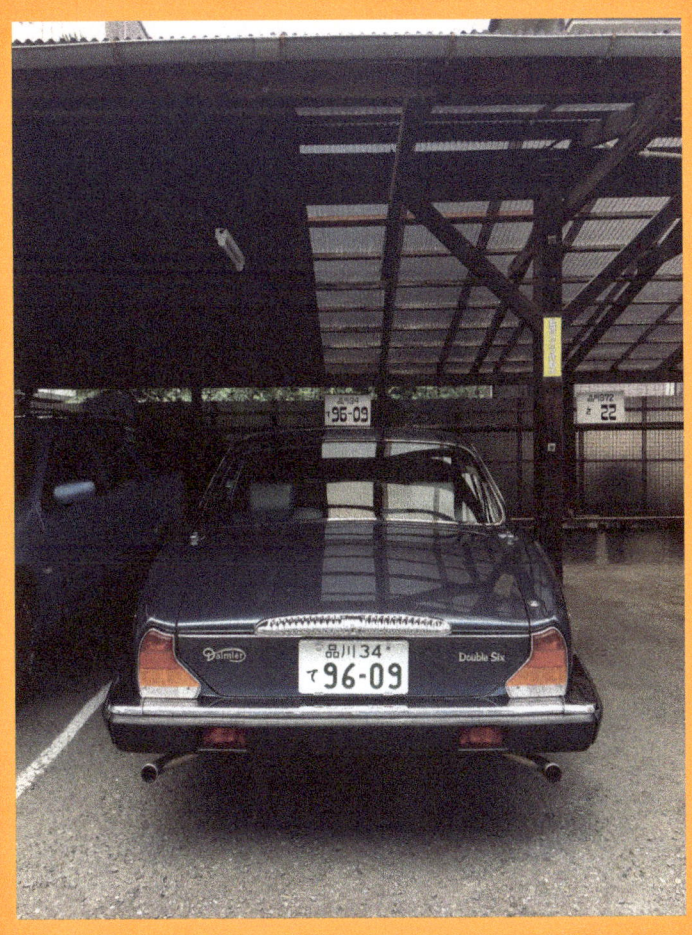

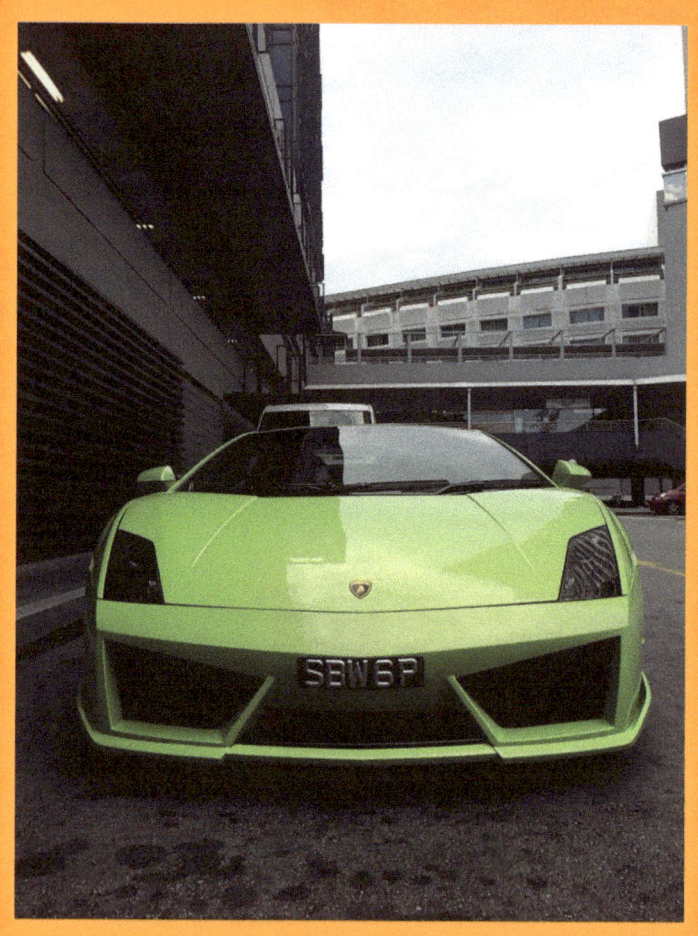

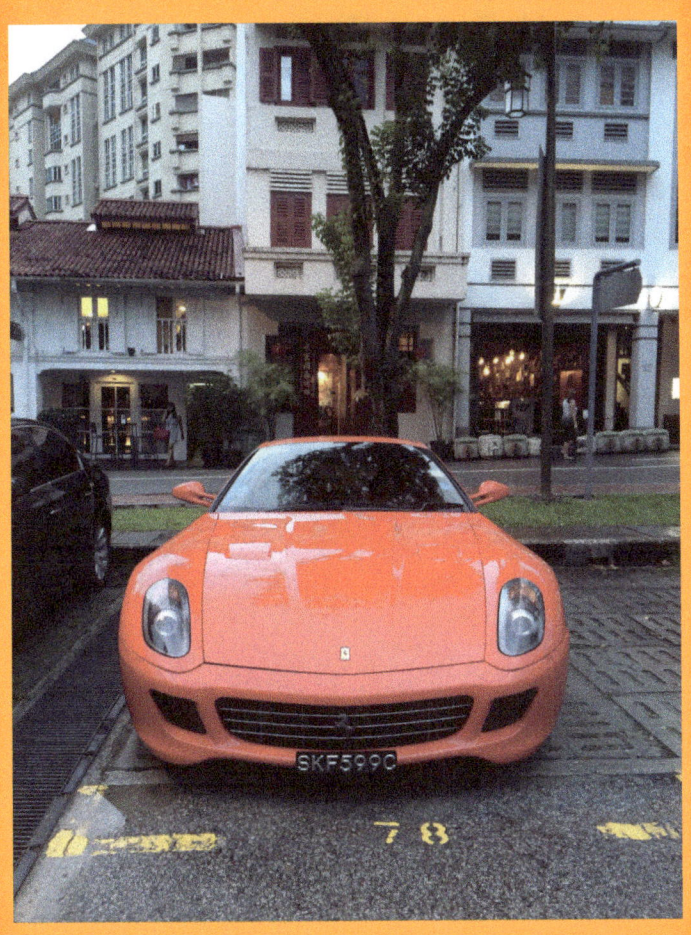

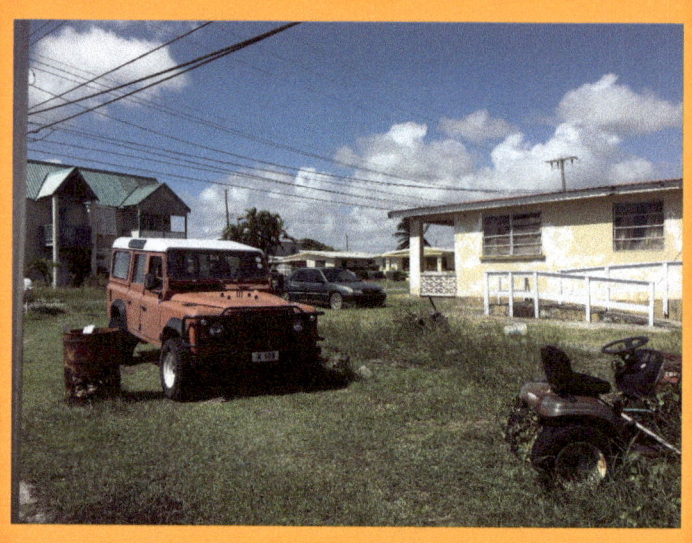

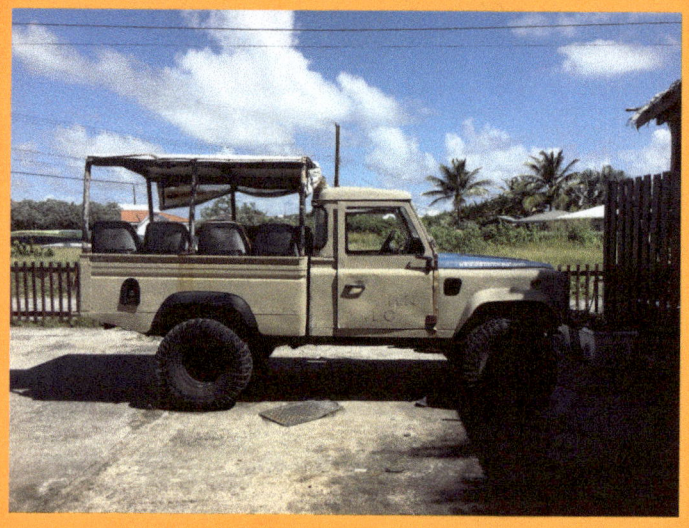

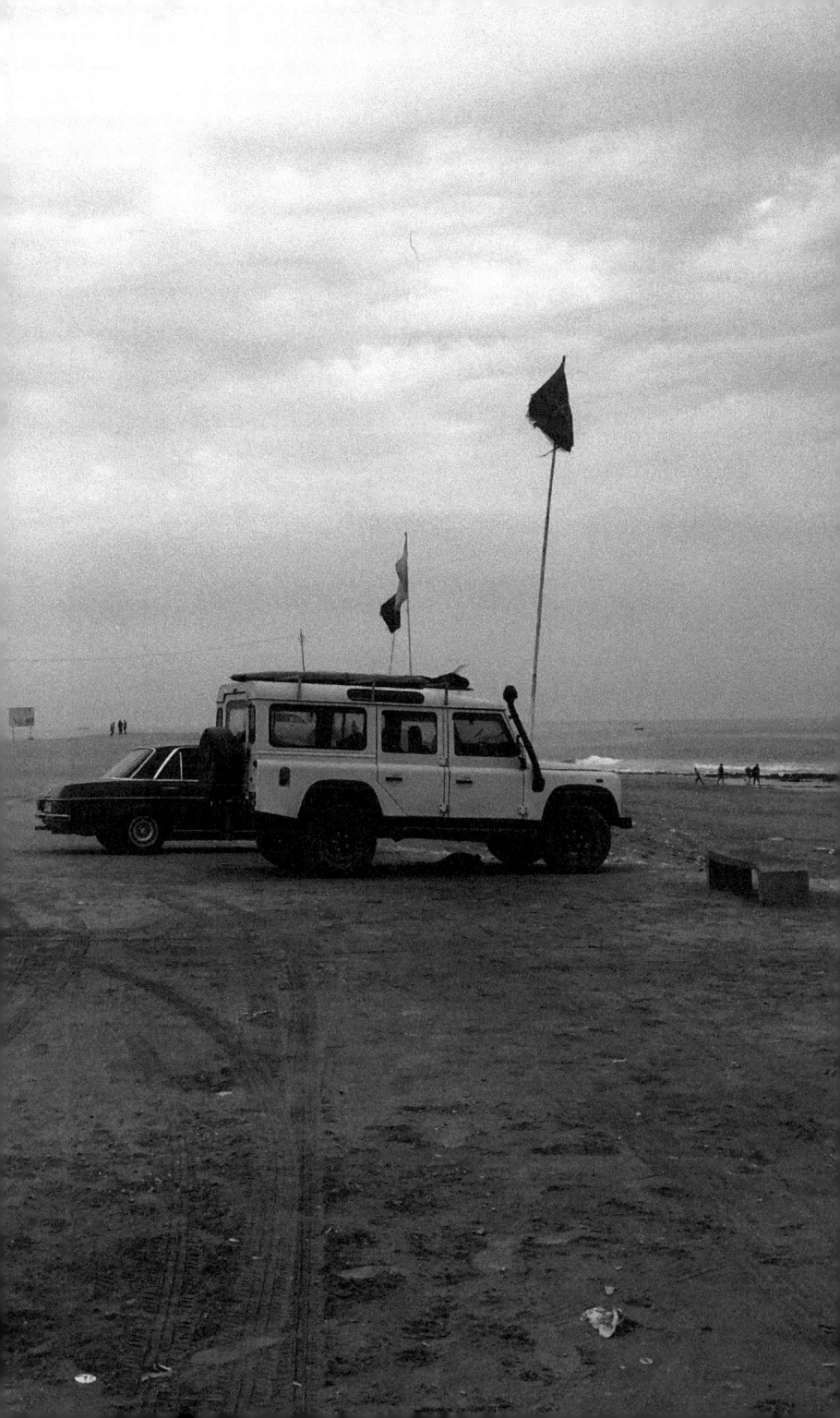

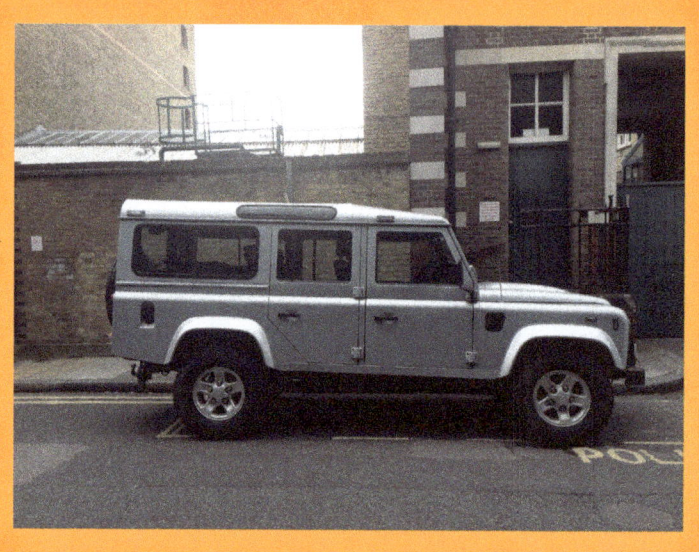

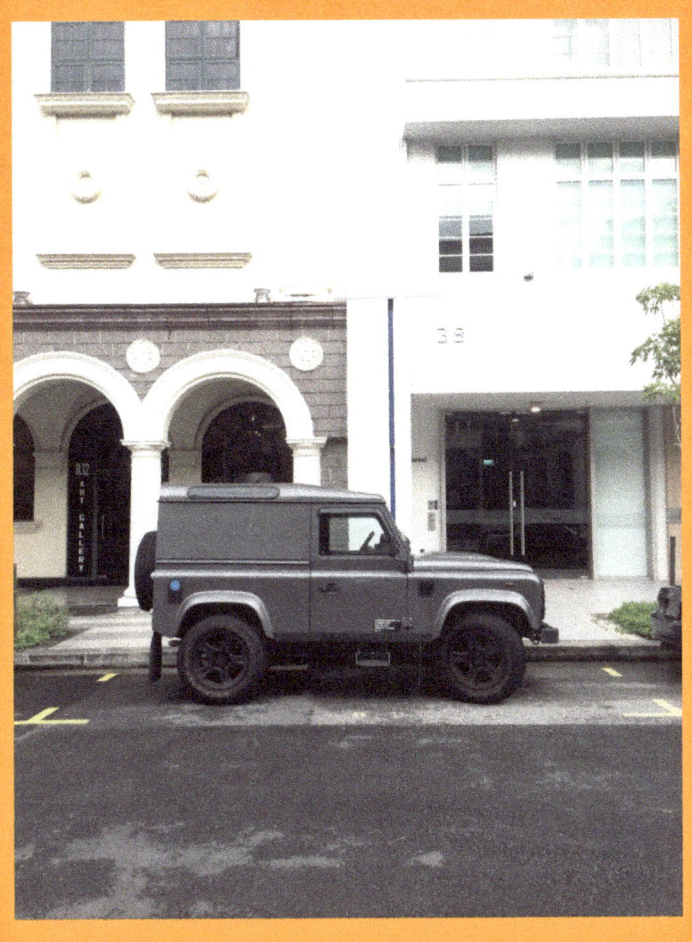

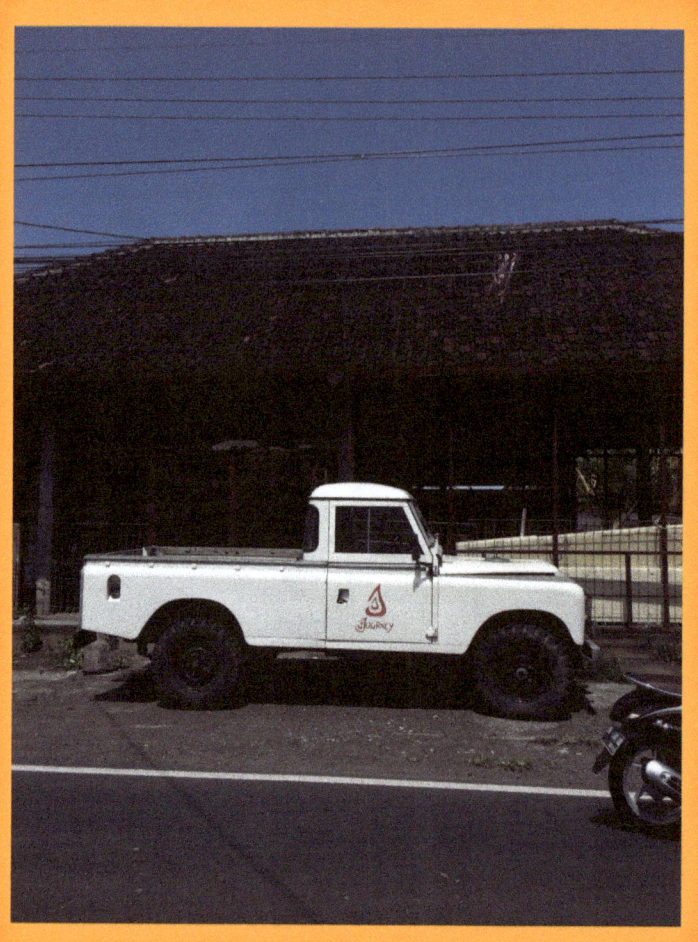

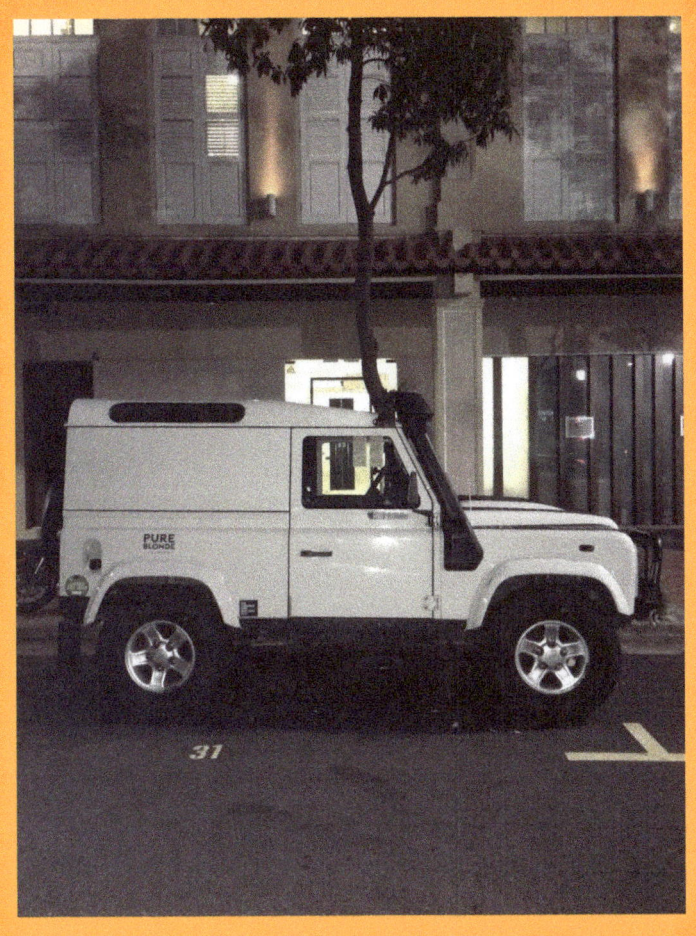

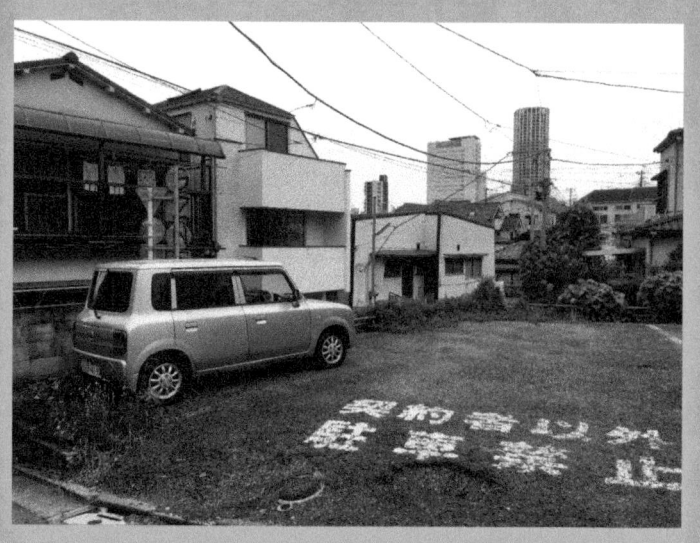

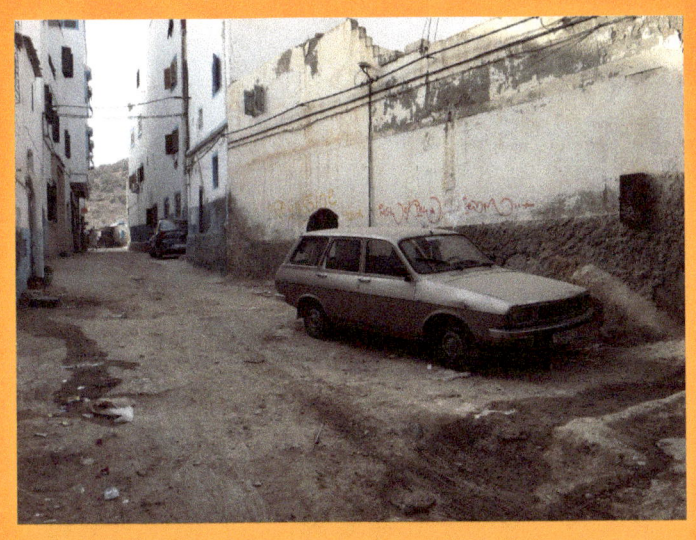

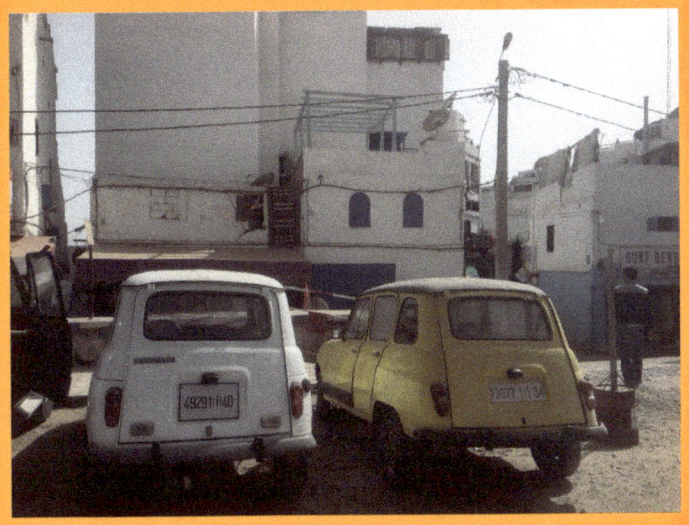

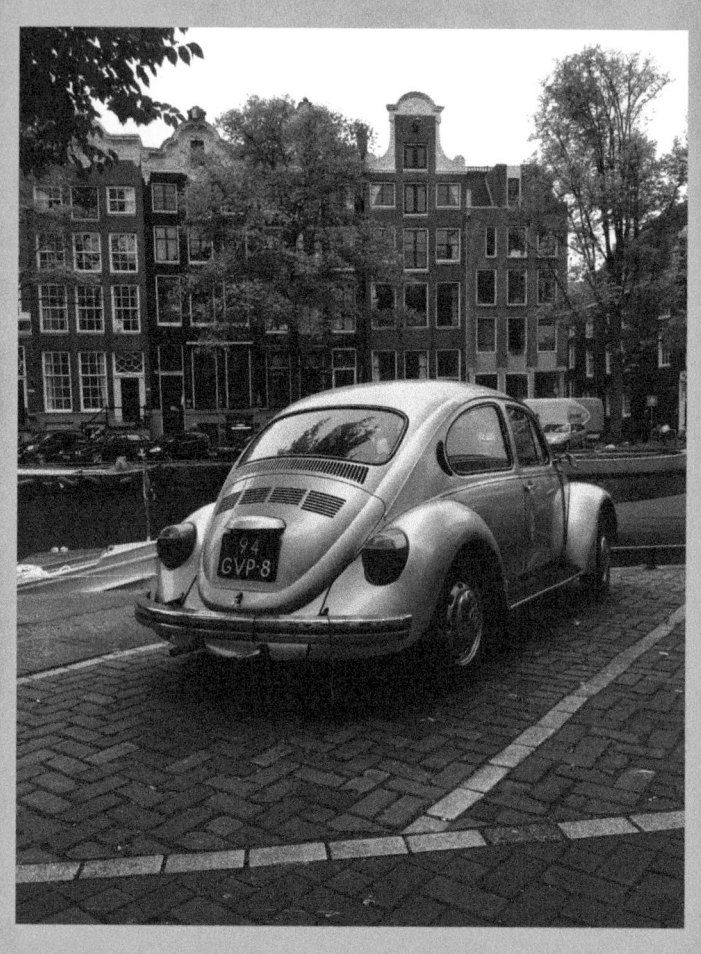

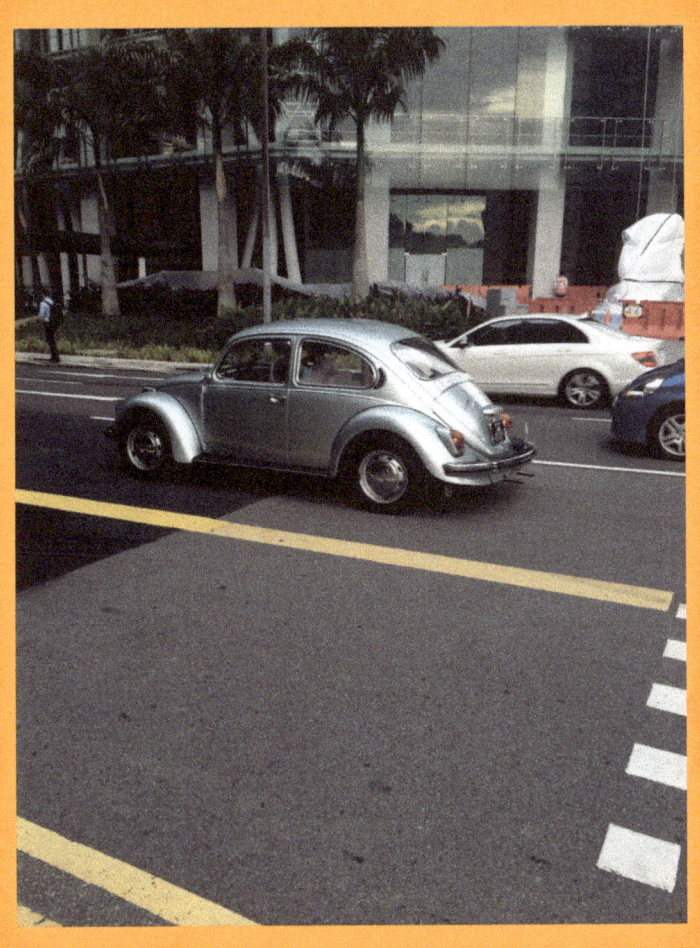

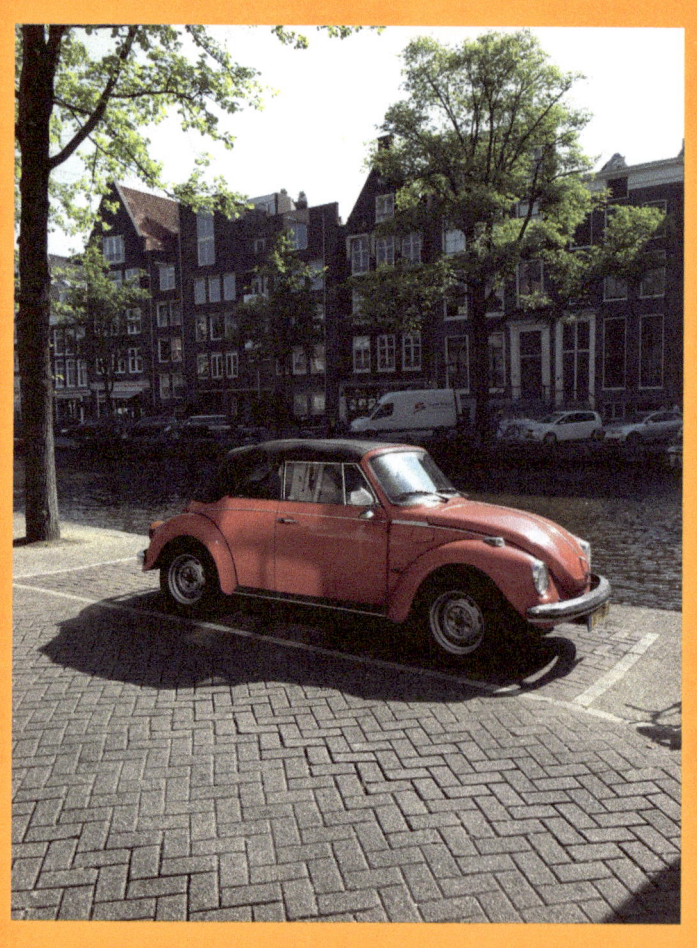

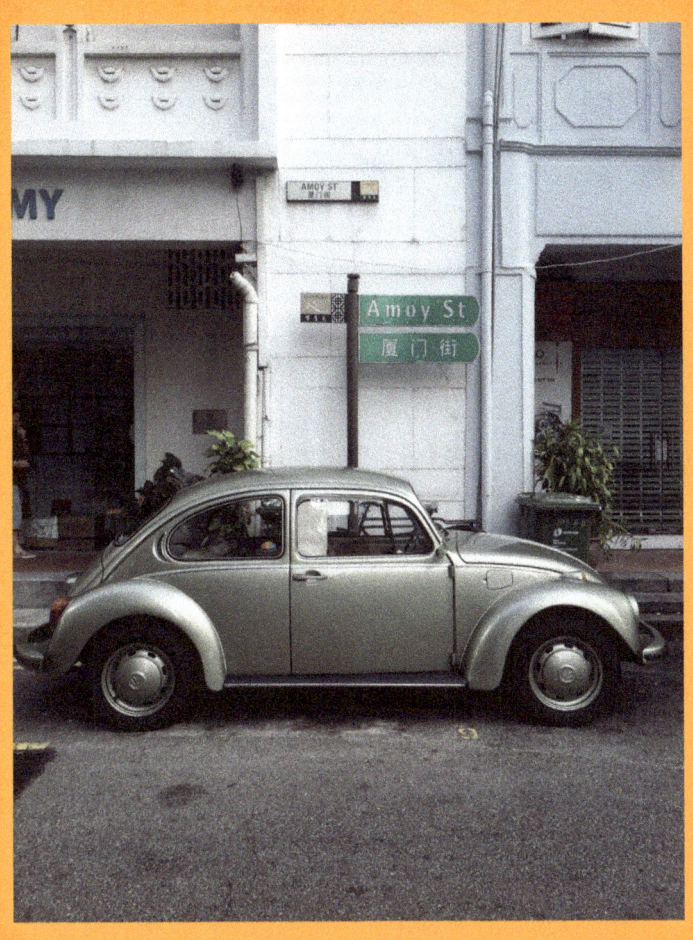

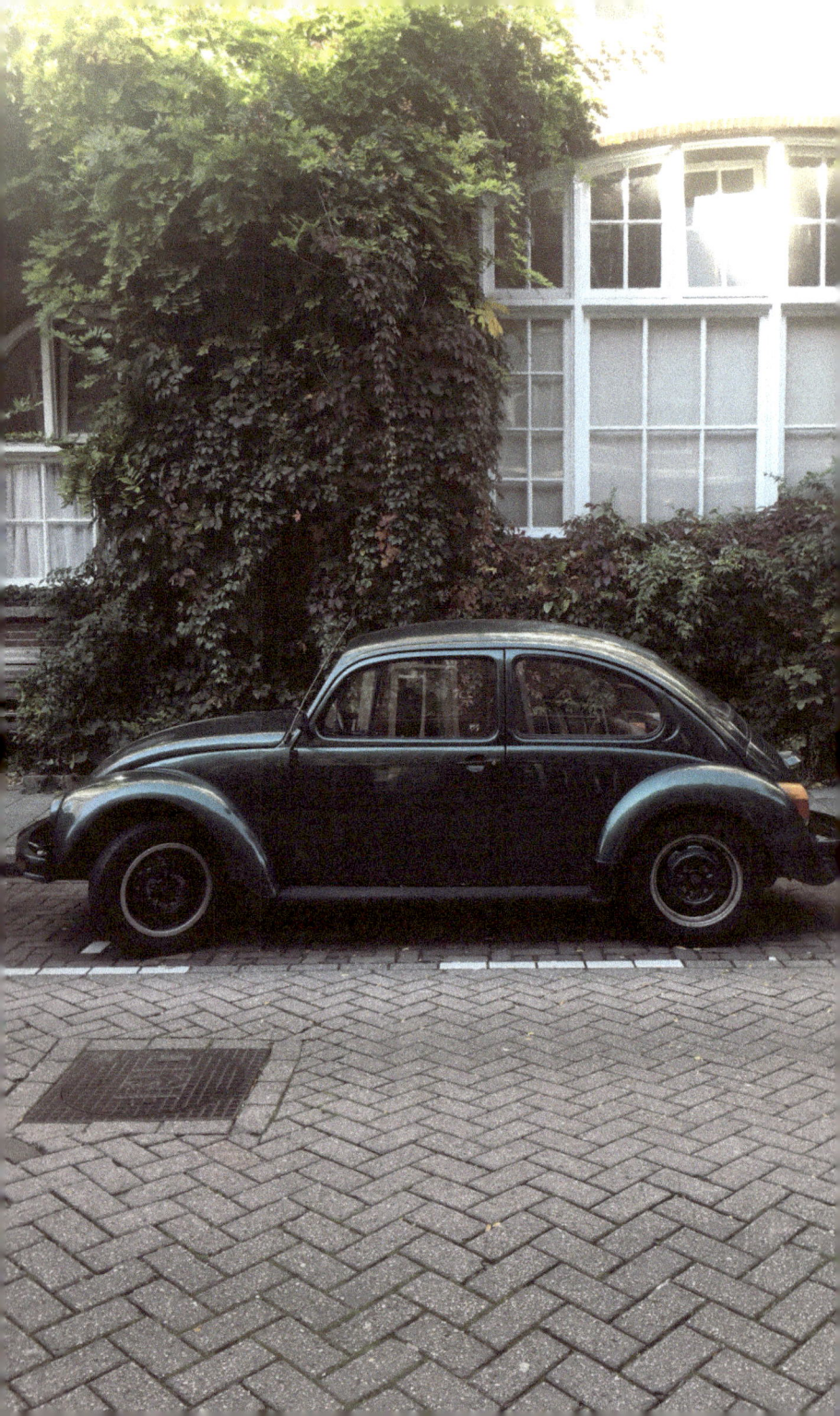

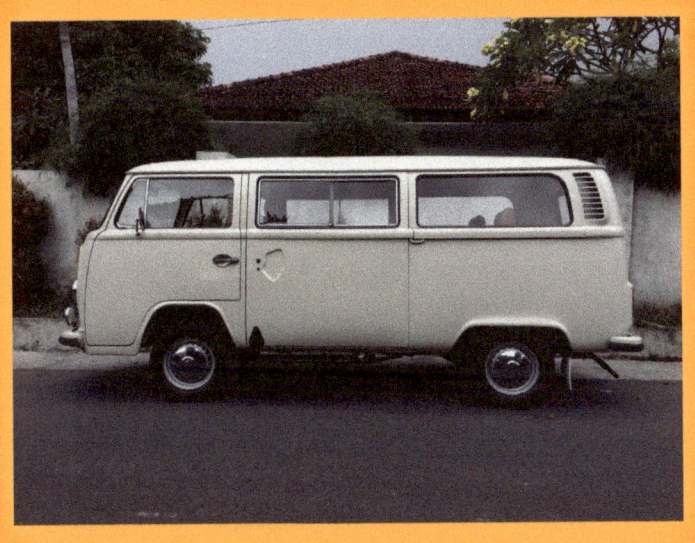

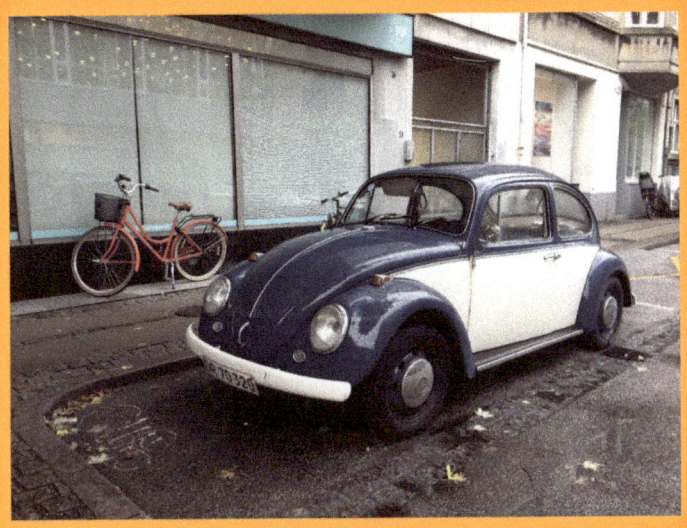

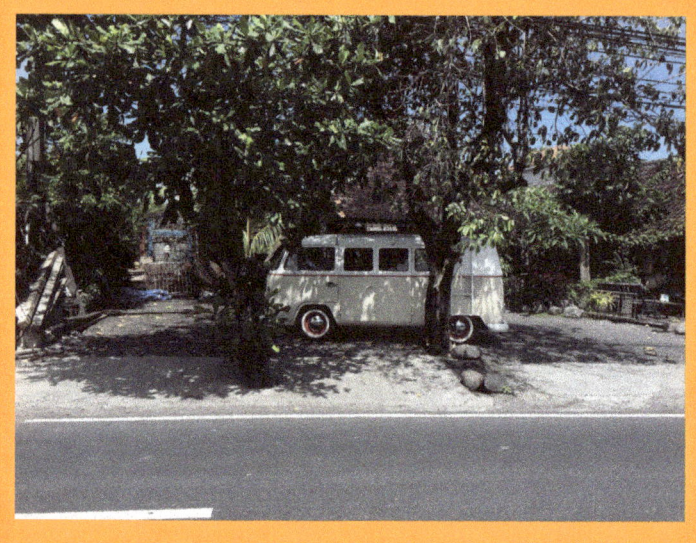

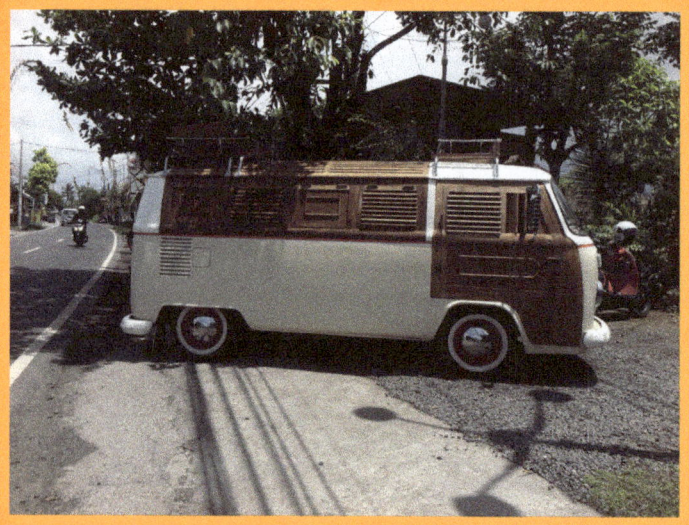

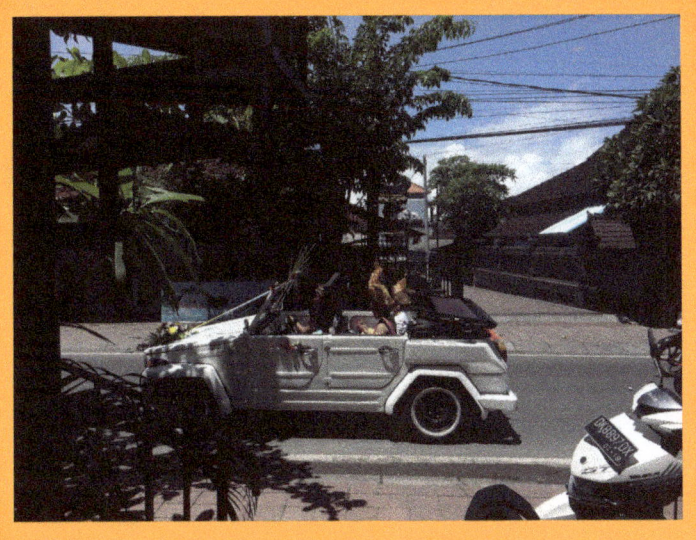

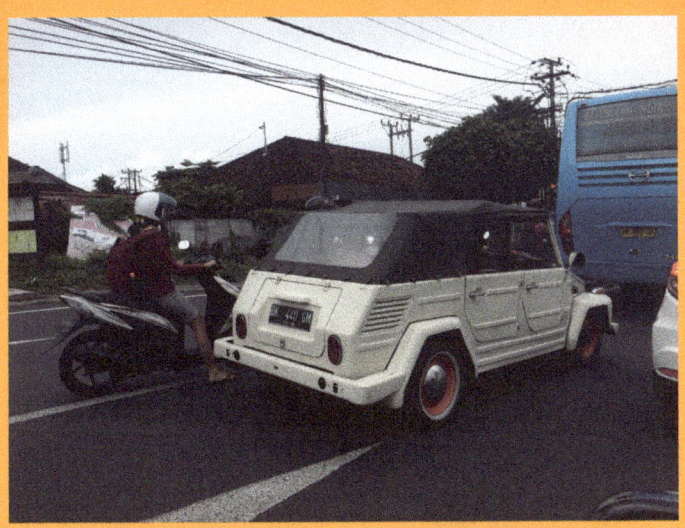

FIN

FIN

FIN

FIN

FIN

FIN

FIN

FAST DON'

FAST DON'T

FAST DON'T

VE FAST DON'T ST

IVE FAST DON'T STO

DRIVE FAST DON'T STOP

DRIVE FAST DON'T STOP

8

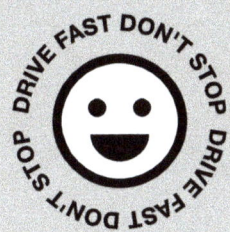

DRIVE FAST DON'T STOP

WWW.DRIVEFASTDONTSTOP.COM

AUTOMOTIVE PHOTO ARCHIVE
BY
MATTHEW JOCELYN

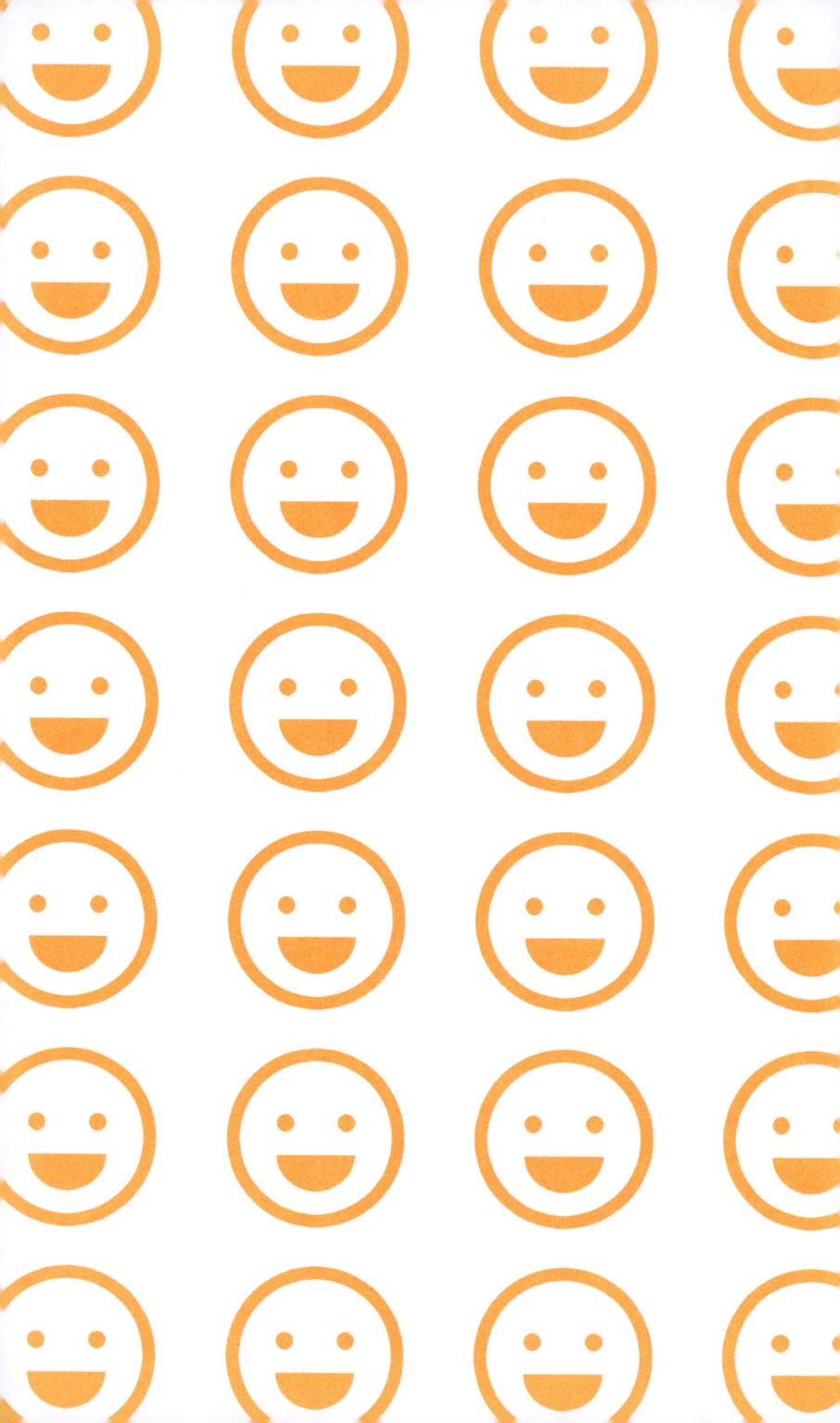

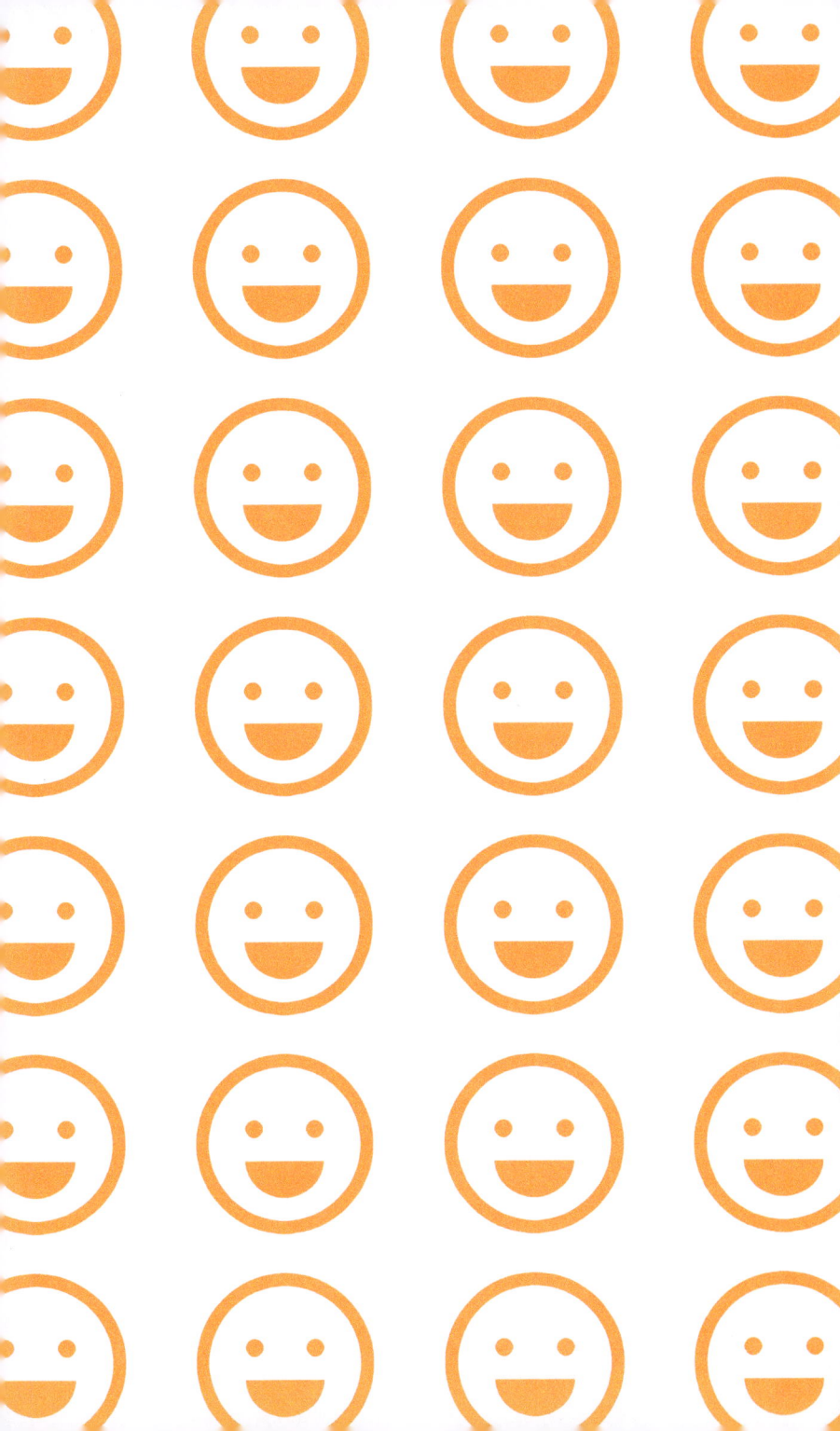

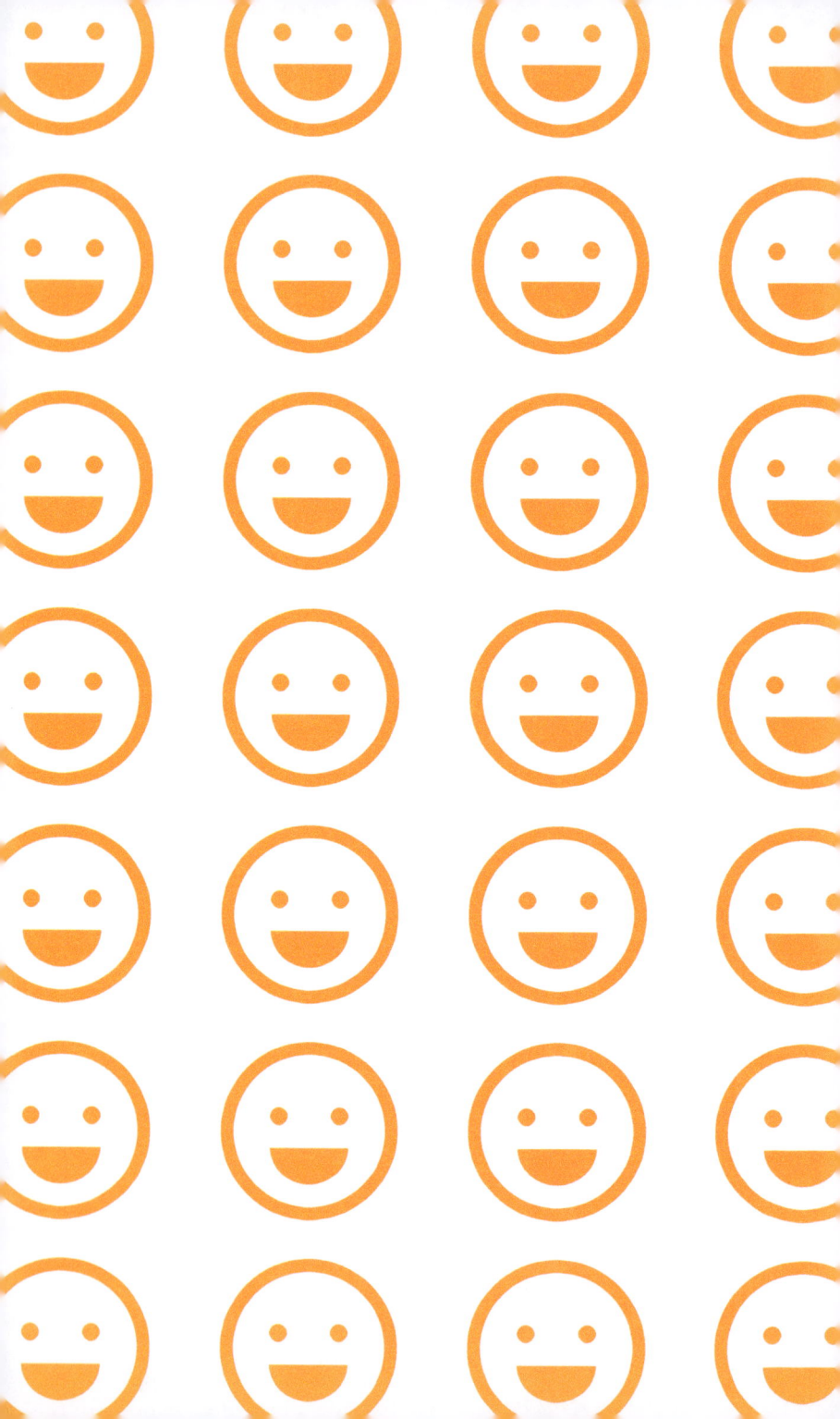